Past Masters
General Editor Keith Thomas

Bayle

Elisabeth Labrousse

BAYLE

Translated by Denys Potts

Oxford   New York
OXFORD UNIVERSITY PRESS
1983

Oxford University Press, Walton Street, Oxford OX2 6DP

London Glasgow New York Toronto
Delhi Bombay Calcutta Madras Karachi
Kuala Lumpur Singapore Hong Kong Tokyo
Nairobi Dar es Salaam Cape Town
Melbourne Auckland

and associates in
Beirut Berlin Ibadan Mexico City Nicosia

British Library Cataloguing in Publication Data

Labrousse, Elisabeth
Bayle.—(Past Masters)
1. Bayle, Pierre
I. Title   II. Series
194   B1825
ISBN 0-19-287541-8
ISBN 0-19-287540-X Pbk

Set by Datamove Ltd
Printed in Great Britain
at the University Press, Oxford
by Eric Buckley
Printer to the University

Contents

Abbreviations

Dict.	*Historical and Critical Dictionary.* All references give the title of the article and the letter designating the footnote, not page-numbers, which differ from one edition to another.
Gen. Crit.	*General Criticism of Monsieur Maimbourg's History of Calvinism.*
Misc. Refl.	*Miscellaneous Reflections on the Comet.*
NLGC	*New Letters by the Author of the General Criticism.*
NRL	*News of the Republic of Letters.* References are to the date and number of the article quoted.
OD	*Oeuvres Diverses*: Bayle's collected works, in 4 volumes. There were two editions: the second is here designated *OD*^{2}, and references are to the volume and page-number. The text is printed in double columns. See also p. 93.
Phil. Comm.	*Philosophical Commentary on the words of Our Lord* ...
RQP	*Reply to the Questions of a Provincial.*

When individual works are quoted, reference is to the title and paragraph number.

1 The background: Protestantism in France

At the end of the seventeenth century many French Protestants were driven into exile, victims of the religious policies of Louis XIV. This dissenting minority found a remarkable and original spokesman in Pierre Bayle (1647–1706), who was to be, in years to come, acclaimed as a forefather of the Enlightenment. Yet everything Bayle wrote can be seen as a direct response to the phenomenon of religious intolerance which reached its apogee in the Revocation of the Edict of Nantes (1685). No proper understanding of his work is therefore possible without an appreciation of the particular character of French Protestantism before that traumatic event.

The intentions of the Protestants in France in the sixteenth century were the same as those of Evangelical Christians in other parts of Europe. Their aim was simply to reform the Church; not to set up a rival institution or start a schism. Although they failed to rally the whole French nation to their cause, they also managed to escape the choice which their counterparts in other Latin countries were forced to make between martyrdom and exile. While they were too weak to win a decisive victory in the long and horrendous series of Wars of Religion (actually civil wars, in which religion was only one factor), they proved strong enough to deny one to their enemies. In the long run, they gained for themselves a number of concessions, of which the most important was simply the right to exist.

Protestantism in France attracted recruits from every social class. It had a particular following amongst the nobility (without whom there would not have been any Wars of Religion). Elsewhere, it drew its strength largely from the urban milieux (taking 'urban' to include, as it normally did in the sixteenth century, the larger villages as well as the towns), where it found supporters among the artisans and, in the towns themselves, among the members of the legal profession, minor royal officials and leading municipal personalities. Geographically, its distribution was very uneven. It flourished in the west and, especially, in the south, in the 'Bible Belt' of the Languedoc, though nowhere were Protestants in the majority. Wherever they were to be found, they rubbed shoulders with Catholics, and whereas the old religion covered the whole kingdom with a close-meshed network of parishes, there were many districts that could not boast even a single Protestant.

A determining factor in the rise of Protestantism in the sixteenth century was the support of a section of the Princes of the Blood, including the future Henri IV. Henri, however, eventually made sure of the throne by abjuring, though he did have the tact to delay his abjuration until the very last moment (1593). The loss of this major political asset was a significant cause of the rash of conversions to Catholicism – the religion of the monarch – which ensued among the nobility in the following century. The most decisive of its many consequences, where French Protestantism was concerned, was a steady growth in the authority of the bourgeoisie and the pastors, particularly once the Edict of Alès (1629) had signalled the failure of the French Protestants' final attempt at armed revolt.

Of all the similar edicts which had preceded it and occasionally brought a brief moment of peace to sixteenth-century France, the Edict of Nantes (promulgated in 1598) turned out to be the longest-lasting. It granted the Reformed Churches the privilege of a legal existence, accompanied by guarantees. Some of these (such as the right to maintain garrisons in certain towns) were only temporary. One, however – that the Edict was valid in perpetuity and would never be revoked – was backed by the Crown's solemn pledge. As a result of the Edict yet another group acquired its place in the sun within the juridical system of the *ancien régime*, which already included a huge number of privileged bodies such as the Catholic clergy, the nobility and a host of towns, corporations, professions and lineages. Logically, this implied that the principle of freedom of conscience was now accepted in France, since there were two officially authorised religions and a Frenchman could legally profess whichever one he wished. But it must be stressed that the idea of the total freedom of the individual conscience, as we understand it today, would have been incomprehensible in the seventeenth century. One proof of this is that the Edict of Nantes applied only to the doctrines, organisation and geographical sphere of influence of the French Reformed Churches, *as things stood in 1598*. There was no provision for any significant evolution of doctrine, any appreciable change in church government or any expansion beyond existing boundaries, and it is clear that had any developments of this sort occurred they would have been looked on as an unacceptable breach of the conditions laid down in the Edict. In other words the Edict was, in more ways than one, a kind of strait-jacket so far as the Protestants were concerned. It froze all their gains and, while providing them with guarantees, forbade them in the same breath to do anything to improve their position or to expand their sphere of influence. This, incidentally, also explains why it was that the Edict did not run in territories annexed to France *after* 1598, where Protestants, if there were any, could only remain if the treaty of annexation had expressly provided for the maintenance of the religious freedom they had previously enjoyed.

Similarly, while the Edict of Nantes may have set out the rights of what were now officially two different religions, it by no means placed them on an equal footing. Right from the start, the status of the French Reformed Churches was hedged around with restrictions. They were not, for example, allowed to have *temples* (churches) in cathedral towns. The rights they enjoyed were fewer than those of the Catholic, Apostolic and Roman religion, which was not only the religion of the king, but also that of the overwhelming majority (some 95 per cent) of his subjects.

The situation of French Protestantism under the Edict of Nantes was unique in Western Europe. Wherever else Protestantism had taken root, it had been under the aegis of the civil power. Many of the idiosyncrasies of the Huguenots can be explained by their status as a barely tolerated minority, which put them in a very different situation from their Calvinist co-religionists in Scotland, the Low Countries, the Palatinate, Geneva or the Swiss cantons. True, they had, on the face of it, the same presbyterian and synodal form of organisation, but the authority of the French consistories was purely moral, which meant that it was precarious and had to be exercised with tact and diplomacy. Not only did their decisions lack the back-up of the civil power, so that excommunication, for example, did not automatically carry with it a civil penalty, but there was nothing to prevent a practising Huguenot from rejoining the majority party if the demands of his Church made life too difficult for him. Indeed, he was constantly being subjected to every kind of insidious social pressure to do so. While the Edict had undoubtedly made it legitimate to profess Calvinism in France, the privilege had to be bought at a high price in both financial and personal terms. Huguenots had to pay tithes to the Roman Church like other Frenchmen; in addition, after the death of Henri IV (1610), their churches rarely received the compensation which the Crown had agreed to give them in exchange, both because of bad faith, and because of the financial difficulties by which the State was constantly beset. As a result, over and above the terrifying roll of taxes and imposts which fell on the shoulders of a seventeenth-century Frenchman, a Huguenot had to pay out of his own pocket for the stipends of the pastors, the upkeep of the buildings and the running of the educational and charitable organisations of his Church. And while younger sons of Catholic nobles could be given ecclesiastical posts, and their daughters taken into convents, neither of these courses was open to the impecunious Protestant nobleman. Protestants, moreover, were subjected to a whole series of discriminatory measures, legal impediments, harassments and, from 1660 onwards, humiliations, which amounted, from the time of the Treaty of Nijmegen (1678), to actual persecution. They were forbidden entry to a growing number of professions, and, what counted for at least as much in the society of the time, prohibited from receiving honours, such as the decorations which the nobles coveted so much, or marks of royal favour and (of particular moment to the bourgeois) access to the highest municipal and judicial offices. It is illuminating to observe how the treatment of the French Protestants resembled that meted out in England to Catholics (or, indeed, between 1660 and 1688, to Dissenters), and to note, for instance, that in France all students at universities had to be Catholics.

As against all this, it should be pointed out that in a number of ways the reformed communities formed an élite. There was less illiteracy amongst them than elsewhere; and the habit of reading the New Testament (even if not always the whole Bible, a large and expensive volume), and of regularly hearing sermons given by pastors who were incomparably better educated and trained than the average Catholic parish priest, provided even the lowliest amongst the devout Huguenots with a solid general culture. Again, a noteworthy sense of solidarity among co-religionists meant that French Protestants looked after the needs of their weaker brethren – the sick, the old, widows and orphans – while their hostility to purely mechanical alms-giving led them to encourage healthy paupers to seek work by providing them with apprenticeships and tools, in much the same way as they provided money to support the studies of poor young men of intellectual merit.

Yet despite superficial similarities, they were very unlike the English puritans (giving the term its widest meaning). Their concern with morality was not an obsession, and they were far from being joyless ascetics tormented by pangs of conscience. Like the original Protestants, their complaint about the Roman Catholics was not so much that they 'lived badly' as that they 'believed wrongly'. They were more concerned that a person's doctrine should be pure, purged of all superstition and idolatry (to use their own favourite terms) than that his conduct should be without stain. It is easy to see, from the sacrifices they were prepared to make for their faith, how psychologically convinced they were of their own salvation: to be loyal to a religion which entailed such temporal disadvantages was for them a clear sign of being in a state of grace. Indeed, was it not written: 'Blessed are they that are persecuted ...'? Their charter, the Code of Discipline of the French Reformed Churches, might forbid the faithful to indulge in dancing, just as it forbade attendance at Catholic services and sermons, but both prohibitions were regularly infringed. Seventeenth-century Frenchmen visibly loved festivities of any kind and when the Catholic bishops and the Consistories of the South, for once on the same side, tried to wean their charges away from dancing, they failed conspicuously, so much was dancing an integral part of traditional celebrations. By the same token, a series of Lenten sermons was a welcome diversion in a small town, while to attend the baptism, marriage or funeral of a Catholic relative or neighbour was a normal part of social life. In all such cases, the Consistories were quite satisfied with a simple word of regret from the offenders, habitual backsliders though they might be. Even when faced with acts contrary to accepted norms of morality, such as sexual offences or assaults against the person, they normally called only for repentance in the sight of the congregation. Their ultimate weapon of refusing the offenders access, temporarily or permanently, to the Holy Communion was something they were reluctant to use.

Where doctrine was concerned, the pastors' main efforts were devoted to attacking the Roman Church with all the acrimony and vehemence normally associated with works of religious controversy. In their daily lives, however, members of the rival churches were often drawn together by close and overlapping bonds of family relationship and physical propinquity, which led laymen of both confessions to live peaceably and in reasonable harmony. There were some social groups that remained very hostile towards the Protestants: the Roman clergy and the rigorist, pro-Spanish, party, and also the magistrature, which had been offended by the patent juridical anomalies of the Edict of Nantes. Outside these groups, however, there were few problems. While each individual naturally regarded his own Church as the best, he did not usually look on it as the only true or the only Christian one. As often as not, he believed that salvation for a man of the other faith was not so much impossible as difficult. Among country-dwellers, the large number of mixed marriages ('patchwork' marriages, as they were called), and the close ties between families, helped to establish a regime of religious tolerance equivalent to that which, at the other end of the social scale, at court, in fashionable drawing-rooms, and in scholarly and literary gatherings, was dictated by good manners. The rampant hostility displayed in the publications instigated by the Revocation of the Edict of Nantes should not blind us to the fact that earlier on an appreciably different situation had prevailed, not of course in the literature of controversy, but in the way people actually lived. Nor did things deteriorate until the authorities began to favour the Catholics systematically and in every sphere of life. This was something which began slowly, then gathered pace after 1660, when it became advantageous to make a show of one's Catholicism and to denounce the Protestantism of an adversary or a rival whenever – and it happened often in an era so punctilious about matters of procedure – professional or social interests were in competition or conflict.

To see the Revocation of the Edict of Nantes (October 1685) as simply the final thrust of the Catholic Counter-Reformation would be misguided. The spate of official justifications of the Revocation may have been couched in the most pompous religious terms, but its decisive causes were political. In every country in Europe, the civil authorities regarded as axiomatic the principle *hujus regio, cujus religio*, from which it followed that it was only rulers who had freedom of conscience. To put it another way, national unity, something so greatly desired at a time when Europe was still a disparate collection of provinces, each with its own dialect, customs and legal system, could not, it was felt, subsist without the bond of religious uniformity. Without going back as far as the expulsion of the Jews and the Moors from the Iberian peninsula at the end of the fifteenth century, which brought about national unity by ensuring religious unity, we need only recall the determined efforts of the Stuarts to rally the peoples of the Three Kingdoms to the Church of England, the national church.

It is easy to understand how the Sun King, at the height of his powers, should in his turn have sought to give his kingdom the benefit of religious uniformity. At first he operated deviously and stealthily, attempting to lure people to Catholicism by making it seem attractive and profitable or, to put it more bluntly, by making Protestantism seem a serious and lasting handicap, as indeed it was, once the tribunals acting under orders gave up even the semblance of impartiality. There were various ways of rewarding those who abjured – the newly converted were, for example, given a moratorium on their debts. The policy in fact brought an uncovenanted bonus to French

Protestantism since it meant it shed some of its fat, losing the socialites and the faint-hearted among its number. There was a sense, then, in which despite a loss of numbers and revenue, it was actually strengthened. On the other hand, those who went over to Catholicism were most often the notables, who had been the biggest financial contributors. Next, some six or seven years before the Revocation, a plethora of decrees of the Royal Council, pursuing what was euphemistically described as a 'rigorous' interpretation of the Edict of Nantes, effectively undermined the basic postulates of the Edict and thus deprived it of all its significance. Looked at from this standpoint, what the Revocation actually did was to consolidate, at a stroke, a process which had been taking place gradually and bit by bit: even before 1685, the number of pastors imprisoned and *temples* 'forbidden' (in other words, destroyed) was legion.

Eventually, in the summer of 1681, the authorities lost all patience and turned directly to the use of force. This was the period of the infamous dragonades, the policy, heartless and brutal in its application, of billeting soldiers on Protestant households, whose inmates were subjected to an odious and costly invasion of their privacy which only ceased when they agreed to abjure. At the same time, it should not be overlooked that the very cruelty and iniquity of the operation contributed powerfully towards rendering it ineffectual, for it imbued its victims with such a hatred of the Catholicism which it was theoretically supposed to be promoting that a large number of Huguenots resigned themselves to leaving their native land, even though long-standing decrees forbade them to do so. The collective term the 'Refuge' first came into use to designate those French Protestants (at least a quarter of a million in number) who managed to escape in secret from France and to set up home in the various Protestant countries of northern Europe, including England, the United Provinces of the Netherlands, and Brandenburg. This first generation of exiles, only gradually assimilated by the host countries, had run enormous risks in escaping (a man could be sent to the galleys, a woman to prison, for life), often leaving behind them the greater part of their possessions. Meanwhile, those Huguenots, notably in the south of France, who had not been able or had not wanted to leave, and who were in the position of no longer being able to be Protestants and yet being compelled to go to church, set up a passive resistance to the Catholicism into which the Revocation forced them, for example by attending Mass but refusing to take communion. Secretly, they were active as well as passive in their resistance, as witness the Assemblies of the Desert, so called because they were held in the open air, and the clandestine reconstitution of the synods after 1715.

To return to Bayle's lifetime, it only remains to point out that whereas the Huguenots were nonconformists in religion, this was not the case in politics. Apart from the fact that they held the Bourbon dynasty in particular affection, having received the Edict of Nantes from Henri IV, who had remained friendly to them even after his abjuration, they were well aware that they could only survive in France given the goodwill of the Crown and its determination to keep the Edict of Nantes in force. This continued to be the situation after 1629, when those southern Protestants who took up arms against the Crown were defeated, thus forfeiting for all French Protestants the right to maintain their own garrisons and other somewhat illusory guarantees which the Edict had temporarily granted them. As for the maintenance of the purely religious privileges accorded to the French Reformed Churches, which Richelieu was politically astute enough not to remove, this depended on the Crown's ability to resist the inevitable and wholly comprehensible demands of the Assemblies of the Catholic Clergy and the pressures brought to bear by the Vatican and the pro-Spanish party. It was thus very much in the Huguenots' interest that the king of France should be sufficiently powerful and well respected to stand firm against the adversaries of Protestantism. Conscious of their dependence on the goodwill of the Crown, French Protestants were, to a man, ardent and unswerving upholders of Divine Right absolutism. Throughout the Frondes, the civil war which raged from 1648–51, the Huguenots as a mass remained faithful to the king. However, partisans of the Revocation (including those who at the time gave it sycophantic approval) persisted in depicting the Huguenots as a threat to political stability and as a foreign body which the monarchy could not assimilate. Relying on an abstract and theoretical image of Protestantism, coloured by tendentious references to the Wars of Religion, they portrayed the Protestants as subversive by nature and by definition, evoking the 'republican' character of their church organisation, based on representative assemblies, the contract theory of political authority canvassed by various Calvinist authors in the sixteenth century and, above all, the recent phenomenon of the English Revolution, which was what alarmed them most. Any sensible ruler, their argument ran, would uproot from his domains a religious body which bore ineluctably within it such an ineradicable tendency to revolt.

Most scandalous of all, from the point of view of the victims of the Revocation, was the betrayal implicit in the abolition of a decree which the Crown had explicitly proclaimed to be binding in perpetuity. (The Edict of Revocation neatly got round this by saying that, there no longer being any Protestants left in France, the provisions of the Edict of Nantes were now obsolete.) Equally scandalous was the fact that Protestants were forbidden to sell up their homes and leave France legally, since this meant that not only were they forbidden to practise their own religion, but that they had publicly to practise Catholicism. The king deliberately avoided imposing a solution on the Spanish model, for everyone in the seventeenth century was aware how greatly it had weakened Spain and Portugal. Rather than expelling the dissidents (apart from some hundreds of pastors who were banished as ringleaders), he endeavoured to prevent them from leaving the country so that he could assimilate them by force. In the majority of cases, he won only sham concessions from them. In a way characteristic of minorities that survive, French Protestantism instilled in its adherents an active sense of community and a keen feeling of religious, moral and intellectual superiority over 'Popery' which they regarded as obscurantist, superstitious and idolatrous. The Huguenots' spiritual pride and their deep fidelity to their traditions kept them going in the seventeenth century despite the patent temporal disadvantages their stand entailed. The same qualities were to sustain them in their resistance to enforced Catholicism in the following century.

2 Bayle the outsider

Pierre Bayle belongs to the transitional group of French writers who unwittingly paved the way for the eighteenth-century Enlightenment. He has suffered from being more talked about than read. The reverence in which he was held after his death by eighteenth-century thinkers has made it too easy to conclude that all he did was to adumbrate some of the themes, such as toleration, anticlericalism and metaphysical scepticism, which they were to make their own. This over-simple, schematic view does not do justice either to the complexity of his thought or to his real historical significance. To appreciate where Bayle stands in the history of French thought, it is important to think of him not just as a sceptic, in the tradition which links Montaigne to Voltaire, but also as a religious thinker, one of a line running from Calvin to Rousseau.

It is not hard to see why Bayle's position has been misunderstood. He noted himself that his writings (which were published between 1682 and 1707) represented something of a throwback to the miscellanies so beloved of sixteenth-century writers. By the same token, they were out of key with the French classical aesthetic which held sway in the Parisian literary milieux of his own day. Bayle wrote essays in the form of letters, and works of high-grade popularisation, aimed at educated readers, which make him one of the founders of modern intellectual journalism. The tone of his writings is subtly polemical, as one would expect of a refugee from persecution, and is all the more effective for the use it makes of irony and understatement. Bayle makes no pretence of being a stylist or an artist, or of writing to a preconceived plan. He writes as people often talk, haphazardly, sharing his knowledge and the things that amuse him, as well as his doubts and his indignation, with his readers. Writing was what he most enjoyed in life, and only incidentally the means by which, as it happened, he was able to earn a modest living.

In his lifetime Bayle was involved in numerous polemics and

in consequence the recipient of a great deal of abuse. He was called not only an unbeliever, but an atheist. In his own environment this was the cruellest insult that could have been levelled at him, but later generations often considered it a term of praise, and turned the imputation of atheism into a compliment. In France, in the heart of a Catholic civilisation, it was particularly easy to see Bayle's criticism of the Roman Church as an attack on Christianity itself. At the root of much of the distortion of Bayle's thought is the fact that he has been read as if he belonged to the milieu of the Regency salons, where unbelief and licentiousness were freely indulged in, whereas such surroundings would have been just about as alien to him (language apart) as the court of the Emperor of China.

Bayle's influence on the eighteenth century highlights the workings of a general rule concerning precursors and their disciples. The disciples are highly selective in their choice of themes from their master's works, transpose them to a new context, and in the process make them into something very different. (The very notion of a 'precursor' must be a highly abstract one, given that it involves describing a man's outlook in terms of ideas which, by definition, he did not know he had.) Nothing operates less mechanically than an influence, and if we want to assess the true originality of those whom it affects, we have to begin by evaluating it on its own terms, and seeing how far posterity has transformed or distorted it.

Early years (1647–68)

In the context of French literature, Bayle is an odd man out in every sense of the term. There can hardly have been a greater handicap than to be born, as he was, provincial, poor and – last but not least – Protestant. Paris (the court as well as the town) was the centre for literary graces, polished manners, intellectual and political life and up-to-date information on everything. It was Bayle's lot to be born (on 18 November 1647) in one of the furthermost parts of France from Paris, a tiny town in the Comté de Foix, at the foot of the Pyrenees. The language he could hear all around him was Occitan, and though French was spoken in the household of his father, pastor Jean Bayle, it was with a thick southern accent which Pierre himself never lost. The family was very badly off, considering its social standing: Pierre's mother came of minor nobility, and his father, by virtue of his profession, was a local dignitary and a scholar. He had studied theology at one of the few places of higher education which the Edict of Nantes had allowed Protestants to set up, the Academy of his native town of Montauban. (Only Catholic establishments could be called universities, while the term academy which the Protestants used was also the word for a riding-school!) Pastors, though, were poorly and irregularly paid, and neither Jean Bayle nor his wife possessed much of a patrimony, just about managing to live off the modest family property which consisted of a kitchen-garden, a few fields, an orchard and a vineyard. Of the many children pastor Bayle's wife brought into the world, only three survived infancy. The eldest, Jacob (born in 1644), was only three years older than Pierre; the two were very close, and took a touching interest in the welfare of the youngest, Joseph (born in 1656). All the boys did occasional work in the garden, helped with the vintage and, sometimes, managed to catch quail in the rocky hills of the surrounding countryside. They lived off the land in an almost medieval way, enjoying life in the open air under the southern sun more, we may imagine, than they did on the dusty school benches. For there was in fact a school in the little town of Le Carla, but only an elementary school, where the Bayle brothers learned reading, writing, arithmetic and the Protestant catechism, after which their father took on their education himself, and introduced them to the rudiments first of Latin, and then of Greek. Thereafter the studious Pierre was let loose on his own on the many books in the pastor's house and those which his father's nearby colleagues were happy to let him borrow. Living like a peasant, and yet speaking French and studying the humanities, his childhood was an odd one by any normal standards.

The Bayle brothers were desperately anxious to imbibe all the knowledge they could by undertaking a regular course of study, but to send them to a secondary school meant finding the money for their board and lodging away from home. Jean Bayle managed to send Jacob, the eldest, to a boarding school that

was linked with the Academy where he had been a student. It
had been transferred in 1660, by royal decree, from Montauban,
a town of some size, to Puylaurens, more of a large village, as
punishment for a skirmish in which Protestant students had
come to blows with pupils of the local Jesuits. However, the
father found it difficult to meet Jacob's expenses even in the
cheapest lodgings, and Pierre was left champing at the bit while
he waited for his brother to finish his studies. His lack of knowledge distressed him, and for the rest of his life he continued to
complain that his early studies had been so haphazard that even
his immense capacity for hard work had not enabled him to
make up the deficiency, or so he felt: 'I regret . . . the time I
would spend studying for six or seven hours without a break,
because I had no method, I only worked at what I felt like
doing, no one took me over the groundwork, and I was always
trying to race ahead and skipping what I should have been doing
in order to get on to what I only ought to have done much later'
(letter to Joseph, 7 Feb. 1675, OD^2 I B 37b). It is hard to think
that Bayle was right about this. Driven on by 'a grim determination and a consuming desire to know everything' (letter to
Joseph, 28 Mar. 1677, OD^2 I B 75a), and prepared to go on
reading indefinitely despite the migraines which were to 'per-
secute' him, as he put it, all his life, Bayle devoured every book
that came his way. His reading included numerous classical
authors, Greek as well as Latin (Plutarch in Amyot's celebrated
translation as well), Montaigne's *Essais* (Bayle's memory was so
prodigious that his friends were later to claim that he knew them
all by heart), and several neo-Latin authors, probably including
Erasmus, but mainly comprising sixteenth-century Protestant
theologians and pamphleteers. Although Pastor Bayle's library
was somewhat austere in its content, and mainly consisted of
books published before 1635, it was by no means to be despised,
despite the absence of atlases and good dictionaries. The
inhabitants of Le Carla were cheerfully unaware of the existence
of the telescope or the hypothesis of the Earth's movement: the
knowledge they revered was confined to the humanities. Pierre
was filled with the desire to master the whole vast domain of
literary culture. Later on, in connection with their youngest

brother, he wrote to Jacob: 'It is a land waiting to be conquered. Show him it ... as God of old showed Moses the land of Canaan, and make him understand not only that he should see it, like Moses, but that he should enjoy it, like Joshua' (letter to Jacob, 9 Feb. 1675, *OD*² I B 40a).

Eventually, in the autumn of 1668, his theological studies at last completed, Jacob Bayle came home to Le Carla to be his ageing father's colleague, whereupon Pierre left for Puylaurens as if he were setting out for Athens in Plato's day. By now, though, at twenty-one, he was five or six years older than the fellow-students with whom he was about to rub shoulders in the philosophy class.

Bayle always regretted the fact that he was half self-educated. As well as making him even more modest than he already was by nature, it affected his character in other ways. It is a reflection of the frustration he felt early on that what mattered most of all to him, as long as he lived, was to indulge his appetite for reading, and his longing to get hold of all the books there were, not for the pleasure of possessing them but for that of handling them, dipping into them, or reading them through. He was never a specialist in the sense that the numismatist, the philologist or the exegetist are, except in bibliography, where he had an astoundingly erudite knowledge of authors and editions. Far from making him want to live more expensively, his long experience of financial stringency taught him to lead a life of almost Spartan frugality, which fitted well with a love of independence that itself was no doubt rooted in the remarkably free life he had enjoyed in his early years, and is reflected in his writings in the individuality of his outlook. When, at a much later date, Bayle's friends set about trying to find him a wife, he evaded their approaches, believing that the responsibilities of a family were incompatible with a life of study – a notion with distant roots in the monastic ideal. He knew many scholars whom 'the experience of domesticity had forced to groan under the yoke of coaching and tutoring' (*Dict.* Palearius n. D). 'A wife, a son, a close relative, if they are seeking material gains or elevation to a post of honour [Bayle himself never had any such ambitions] never leave a man of letters alone: they insist that he solicits, intrigues or curries favour on their behalf, and when he refuses, they chide him and pick quarrels with him' (*Dict.* Melanchthon n. H). In study, on the other hand, Bayle claimed to find 'as much pleasure and happiness as others do at the gaming-table or in the tavern' (letter to Cuper, 1 Dec. 1692, *Romanic Review*, xxiii, 1932, 23). Like everyone with a consuming passion for work, he enjoyed being alone, and was never happier than when completely absorbed in his books and his papers. On the other hand, he did not shun human contact, for if he was not much of a conversationalist, he was a prolix writer, and it was through writing that he kept up a constant, living relationship with an unseen audience made up of the recipients of his letters and the unknown readers of his books. He was not at all introverted or morose, and no enthusiast for purely abstract thought, as his total inability to cope with mathematics shows. The spontaneous, picturesque way in which he writes is an accurate reflection of the informal and unregulated nature of his early studies. As he himself acknowledged: 'I have no idea what applying myself consistently means; I get sidetracked very easily; I often lose sight of my subject; I skate over potential difficulties; I am the kind of person who drives to distraction the scholar who expects method and consistency' (*Misc. Refl.* i).

In search of the true Church: Toulouse (1668–70)

Standards in philosophy at Puylaurens were distinctly low. This was only to be expected since the subject was taught to children of fourteen and fifteen, who were mainly expected to show how good they were at juggling with syllogisms. While it was clearly a misfortune for any teacher to have someone of Bayle's mature years, sharp mind and eager curiosity as a pupil, he himself was bitterly disappointed after having looked forward so long and so passionately to sitting at the feet of people of real authority. Without telling his family, at the end of three months he left for the Catholic metropolis of Toulouse, where a Jesuit college of good academic standing took in Protestant day-boys. As was inevitable, the young Bayle went over to Catholicism (on 19 March 1669), as a result of being beaten in argument by a priest on the subject of the true Church. His immediate reward was a small grant which solved his material problems and, indeed, he stood to gain so much temporally that, had his Catholicism lasted, self-interest would clearly have seemed the obvious explanation for the change. In fact, Bayle's religious faith was unshaken: all he was seeking was a way of practising it that was more in conformity with God's commands. He had been converted intellectually, as the result of his failure to find convincing arguments with which to counter the traditional case against the Protestant Reformation. It was as if a mathematician were to correct an error of computation. Even so, his action took moral courage as well as intellectual honesty, and had the occasion been different it was the sort to have delighted his father, who had brought him up to obey God rather than man, even if this meant ignoring the claims of kith and kin. Inevitably, however, it led to a breach between Pierre and his family, who were deeply grieved by his 'revolt' (as the Huguenots called the action of anyone who left their ranks).

Gradually the new convert became scandalised at heart by the 'excessive homage' which the Church of his adoption appeared to pay to creatures rather than to the Creator. The Jesuits of Toulouse were no doubt exaggeratedly devout in the Spanish manner, but even without that, the adoration of the Blessed Sacrament would have been enough to shock the religious sensibility of an erstwhile Protestant. More and more the young man began to regret his hasty decision, something that those left behind at Le Carla had been expecting, since they had never supposed that his conversion had been due to self-interest, and were eagerly awaiting the return of the lost sheep to the fold.

This was easier said than done. Most of the articles of the Edict of Nantes had already been abrogated by decrees of the Royal Council, and it was now a serious crime to abandon the religion of the Catholic and Apostolic Church of Rome. After a brilliant defence of his MA thesis in August 1670, Bayle left Toulouse secretly and fled to the town of Mazères where, at night, at a quiet ceremony attended by a number of pastors, including Jacob who had come from Le Carla to see his brother for what was to be the last time, he returned to the religion of his fathers – not without a touch of euphoria, as can be seen from a letter written shortly afterwards. Then, with a bad mount and only a few coins in his pocket, he made haste to Geneva, arriving there safely on 2 September 1670.

Bayle was now on his own on the high roads of Europe, cut off for ever from his family and his native province. However, his experience had taught him a lesson that was lost on the majority of his contemporaries, namely that it was possible to persist in an 'erroneous' belief and still be wholly sincere and disinterested. Today, when we are all relativists, this is obvious. But in the seventeenth century it seemed subversive and scandalous. Nearly everyone was content to believe that, apart from the backward and the uneducated who knew no better, those who adhered to a 'false' Church were acting in bad faith and stubbornly refusing to listen to the voice of conscience.

Full of zeal as a result of his return to the Protestant fold, Bayle was keen to become a pastor, though there was little likelihood that someone who was *persona non grata* in France and even somewhat suspect to his own co-religionists, thanks to the Toulouse episode, would ever find a parish. For eighteen months the situation remained static. Meanwhile Bayle obtained a post in which he lived *au pair*, board, lodging and laundry all found, with a Genevan family. While his charges were at school, he followed the courses at the Academy and went to adult lectures given by the professor of philosophy, an enthusiastic Cartesian who became a great friend and won Bayle over to the new philosophy, which he had previously encountered only through hearing it refuted by his Aristotelian teachers at Toulouse. Bayle also read voraciously. For the first time in his life he had access to the most recent works of French literature, novels, plays, poetry, and also newspapers. His Latin, thanks to the quantity of sixteenth-century authors he had read at home, was somewhat lacking in Ciceronian elegance, and this again he remedied at Geneva, helped by his friendship with an undergraduate contemporary, the Frenchman Jacques Basnage, and with a young Genevan pastor; both were good humanists, steeped in the classics and sworn enemies of scholastic pedantry.

Although naturally thrifty, Bayle needed money, if only to buy clothes, but the French invasion of the United Provinces caused taxes to rise so steeply that it was clear that he could no longer expect to receive anything from his family at Le Carla. In May 1672 he took a salaried post as tutor to the son of the comte de Dohna at the family seat of Coppet. This was some distance from Geneva and meant giving up his studies at the Academy, but the appointment showed how well his Genevan professors thought of him: it was they who had recommended him to the aged Prussian aristocrat, a close relative of William of Orange and of the Elector of Brandenburg who was a fervent Protestant and a great friend to the little republic of Geneva.

Bayle's stay at Coppet, between May 1672 and May 1674, initiated him into polite society and into politics. Dohna had detested Louis XIV even before he was half-ruined by the confiscation of his French wife's property, and he was well informed about recent European diplomatic history, thanks to the posts he had held and to his family connections. He gave the benefit of his views to Bayle, who was shrewd enough to be able to separate hard fact from partisan commentary. Again, while the Dohna family, as Protestants, were not particularly worldly, their drawing-room was none the less a place where a young man up from the country could learn to polish his no doubt rough manners. Bayle took a passionate interest in current affairs and was an avid reader of the newspapers available in Geneva, not only the French gazettes which idolatrised Louis XIV but also the Dutch periodicals which took the opposite stand. It took time for the latter to reach Coppet, but when they did the effect was to reinforce the pro-Dutch sentiments of the Dohna household. Bayle learned, from this contact with diametrically opposite points of view, to play the impartial spectator of a scene about which he had contradictory feelings. As a faithful subject of his sovereign, he was secretly proud when the French armies began to win battles, while as a Protestant he was anxious that the United Provinces should stand firm against the invader.

Valuable as the experience was, there was no future for Bayle at Coppet. In any case, as a Frenchman, he was eager to visit France north of the Loire and especially Paris, where intellectual life was at its peak. His friend Basnage had become pastor at Rouen and got Bayle a post as a tutor in Normandy. Police methods were still in their infancy, and there was little chance of Bayle's being identified as a lapsed Catholic so far from his own province, but to be on the safe side he changed the spelling of his name for a time to Bèle. In June 1674, after passing through Paris, he disembarked at Rouen. A few months later he went one better and obtained a post in Paris itself as tutor to an aristocratic Protestant household. Unfortunately for him, the post proved to be exceptionally demanding. His pupils did not go to school, and he was 'condemned to stay in his room like a tortoise in its shell' (letter to Joseph, 26 June 1675, *OD*^{2} i B 47a). He had no chance to make use of the good offices of Huguenot men of letters, who would have introduced him to scholars accustomed to welcoming young people to their gatherings. It was all very different from the semi-patriarchal atmosphere of Coppet. Arrogantly treated and badly paid, Bayle felt humiliated. It seemed as if, at twenty-eight, the future held nothing for him.

Sedan (1675–81)

However, Bayle still had a guardian angel in Basnage, who deserves the thanks of posterity for recognising his friend's exceptional gifts and making sure that they found an outlet. It was from Basnage that Bayle learned that the Protestant Academy of Sedan was holding a competition for one of its philosophy chairs, and it was Basnage who pushed him into being a candidate. Risking his all, Bayle set out for the Ardennes. He won the competition, not simply because of the excellent grounding the Toulouse Jesuits had given him, but also because outsiders were put off by the meagre salary offered and local candidates were mediocre. Materially, Bayle's situation was not much better than at Paris. He still had very little money, and was forced to borrow against the expectation of his first year's salary. He was still overworked, since he made himself write out his lectures in full, partly because he was conscientious, but also because he was not a fluent orator. Psychologically, though, the difference was considerable. No longer a lowly tutor, he had adolescents and not impossible aristocratic brats as his pupils, and he occupied an honourable position in the large Protestant community at Sedan, where his affable nature and moral integrity won him the esteem of everyone and made him some good friends. Although he was a convinced Cartesian, he was obliged by the syllabus to expound the philosophy of Aristotle. Like most of his colleagues at this particular juncture, he used his lectures to try to put the new wine of corpuscular physics into the old bottles of scholasticism, although in logic (taught, as everywhere in Europe, in the first year) he kept to traditional paths. He kept on revising the first draft of his lectures, but once this was done he had time to spare, and inevitably set about indulging his appetite for books, which he borrowed from the professor of theology, Pierre Jurieu, to whom Basnage had recommended him. Jurieu was ten years older than Bayle and became his protector and patron. He was cultivated, clever and enthusiastic. Bayle became personally attached to him as a stimulating friend and companion who brought a ray of sunlight into his life at Sedan. Jurieu, however, showed more than a touch of condescension in playing the part of mentor to his young colleague. He had a good library, and private means which enabled him to buy a great many books, so that Bayle was able to read, soon after they were published, the works of Spinoza (1632–77) and Malebranche (1638–1715), men who, although deeply influenced by Cartesianism, were profoundly original thinkers and the two most important European philosophers of the period. Bayle also devoured the writings of many other philosophers, now long-forgotten, who attempted to reconcile Aristotelianism and mechanistic physics in what was known as 'la philosophie novantique'.

It was after he left Toulouse that Bayle discovered that he had gifts as a letter-writer. The impulsive style so characteristic of his subsequent literary work is already in evidence in the long, lively and good-humoured letters in which he passed on to his family in Le Carla extracts from his gleanings of books, newspapers and conversations. Almost everything that he eventually wrote, whether in letter form or not, was set down as the ideas came into his head, without much of a plan, just as if he were writing to a close friend.

Sedan saw the beginning of Bayle's literary career, with the composition of a highly technical set of objections to a work by Pierre Poiret, a Cartesian pastor with strongly mystical leanings, and a satirical pamphlet on the Affaire des Poisons, undiscovered and unpublished until the twentieth century. In this work, Bayle contrasts two points of view, ascribing each to an imaginary interlocutor, and leaves the reader to draw his own conclusions. He was to adopt this procedure, reflecting his sense of the fundamental complexity of things, in many of his writings. At this embryonic stage of his literary career, Bayle was gaining practice in two departments in which he was to excel: powerful critical analysis combined with dialectical brilliance in the objections to Poiret, and biting irony together with acute observation in the satire, which was directed at a compromised aristocrat, the maréchal de Luxembourg.

Louis XIV's religious policies were now beginning to spell increasing danger for the Huguenots, and decrees of the Royal Council were continually nullifying what little effectiveness the Edict of Nantes still enjoyed. Following the Peace of Nijmegen (1678–9), the French Court was able to turn its attention to home affairs and move further towards the ideal of making France 'wholly Catholic'. When Sedan had become part of France by treaty with the duc de Bouillon, the Protestant majority had been guaranteed freedom of religion, but Louis XIV did not let this stand in his way, and in July 1681, at the same time as the first dragoons were descending on Poitou, the Academy of Sedan was abolished by a stroke of the royal pen.

The Refuge in Holland

To the more perspicacious Huguenots, it was clear that the avalanche of Royal decrees spelled the imminent abrogation of the Edict of Nantes. When the Sedan Academy was suppressed in spite of the existence of legislation ostensibly protecting it, several of its professors decided to leave France. Bayle, who was the poorest of them, had to find a source of income without delay. Just as he was contemplating trying his luck in England, where the aristocracy had the reputation of behaving generously towards the continental tutors they regularly engaged for their sons, news came that one of his former pupils, a young Dutch patrician, had proposed to the burgomasters of Rotterdam, one of whom was his uncle, that they should expand the town's 'École Illustre' – a euphemistic title since the educational establishments which went under that name did not enjoy university status. A chair of philosophy and history was created for Bayle, and one in theology for Jurieu, who was to be the francophone Walloon community's second pastor. At this time, the law of 1669 which forbade Huguenots to leave France was not being applied at all rigorously, as it was to be later when the tide of refugees became a flood and the authorities reacted by making it impossible for them to leave except in secret, and at the risk of severe punishment if they were caught. Bayle reached Rotterdam without difficulty in October 1681. This was the end of his wanderings. From now on, he never left the Dutch port except for occasional sorties to neighbouring towns such as The Hague, Leiden or Amsterdam, and a single visit to the spa of Aix-la-Chapelle.

The community of which Bayle now became a member had a character of its own. Already when Bayle arrived in Rotterdam there were enough French refugees in the town for him to be able to find lodgings in a French-style boarding house. There he slept in sheets, not simply on a feather mattress, and drank wine rather than beer; he could avoid pipe-smoke, guaranteed to give him headaches, and could warm himself at an open fire instead of by a stove. All these little details made the change of surroundings less disconcerting and painful. Exile was made even sweeter by the arrival, in the years that followed, of thousands more refugees. Bayle never needed to learn Dutch. French was already the second language, spoken by the Walloon minority, and the arrival of the Huguenots strengthened its position. In lectures, and when communicating with the handful of scholars who knew no French, Bayle used Latin. To a southerner like Bayle, Rotterdam cannot have seemed too different from Sedan as regards climate, customs and scenery. The influx of refugees had led to the establishment of further

Walloon churches, which gave the Huguenots what they sought above all else in going into exile, the freedom to practise their religion in the way they had been accustomed to do in France.

However, it should be stressed that the Huguenots were not convinced expatriates. They went on looking forward to the day when they could return to France without stigma, and it was a long time before they were prepared to accept that the French authorities had no intention of abandoning the religious policy on which they had embarked. Many of those who fled had been so sure of being able to return that they had left behind not only property, but family, notably the aged, womenfolk and young children. Meanwhile, the hospitable attitude of the Walloon communities and the lack of a centralised administration in the United Provinces militated against any friction the refugees' exclusiveness might otherwise have caused. A prosperous economy made it easy for the newcomers to find work and for the less favourably situated among them to benefit from Dutch generosity. Amongst the nobles, some lost that status in French law by resigning themselves to working, but most took service as soon as they could in the armies of William of Orange.

Exile removed all Bayle's earlier handicaps. Although uprooted from his family, he was back amongst his fellows, most of whom were poor like himself. His personal odyssey had caused him to by-pass the centres of French culture, but at Rotterdam he was right in the heart of a francophone, Huguenot subculture to which, paradoxically, the Revocation of the Edict of Nantes was about to give a fresh stimulus. Although Huguenot writers had been more or less tolerated in France, they had been obliged to tread warily in order not to compromise the mass of their co-religionists. Such self-censorship was unnecessary in exile, and they soon discovered the heady delights of freedom of expression, less unconstrained, naturally, than we are used to in the West today, but exceptionally liberal for the period, especially in comparison with France, where the authorities exercised a tight censorship. As a result, a number of exiled writers, with Bayle in the forefront, wrote with a degree of boldness to which their readers were so unaccustomed that some were upset by such 'impertinences'.

It was the educated refugees who benefited most from their new surroundings. The Netherlands were already a highly active centre for publishing, and much that was printed there was in French. This was even more the case following the great influx of refugees who became not only authors and proof-readers but also potential purchasers, particularly of literary and political journals, and ephemera such as cheap political pamphlets with news from France, which the refugees eagerly awaited. In choosing Rotterdam as his destination, Bayle had hit upon a bookseller's paradise, where there was no difficulty in finding a publisher, or a public, for his books. It is piquant to note that it was not readers in France who were responsible for the instant success of this French author; their support only came later.

It would be hasty to conclude, however, that all was now well for Bayle and his fellows. They had gone into exile of their own free will, it is true, and had found freedom there, but one has only to think of today's displaced persons to appreciate that the experience was still a traumatic one. As time went on, and there was no sign of an end to what they had originally imagined would only be a temporary state of affairs, the refugees became increasingly depressed and weighed down by a sense of temporal failure. The bitterness and the quarrels which, as we shall see, were to tear them apart were the natural consequence of the feeling that they had been thrown into the dustbin of history as a result of events over which they had no control, and that, cut off from a past which they idealised and cherished, they had no future either. It took some time for them to realise that they could not for ever remain both Protestant *and* French, and that in going into exile in order to preserve this dual identity, they had in fact lost it, for in a matter of a few generations their descendants, although still Protestant, would no longer be French. Furthermore, as well as giving them protection and shelter, the Walloon communities also provided them with an environment in which they could not help meeting people from other milieux and even other provinces, and so gave them the incentive to enlarge their horizons beyond the bounds of famliy and native region. Exile notoriously makes a man aware of himself as an individual and gives him a sense of the relativity of things, lending his life and outlook something of the picaresque. It was in this spirit that Bayle, along with some of his readers and disciples, set off on a voyage of intellectual adventure, while the Refuge itself was, more generally speaking, a place of cultural ferment from which at least part of the ideology of the Enlightenment was to arise.

Rotterdam, early publications, family tragedy (1681–6)

Although poorly paid, Bayle's post at the École Illustre was largely a sinecure: he had only to put in as many hours in a week as he had in a day at Sedan. After ten years in which most of his time had been spent in earning enough to live on, Bayle was once more able to enjoy life as he had in the first flush of youth, and to devote himself almost entirely to his own studies. As well as continuing to devour every book that came to hand, he now began to write for publication. Among the few personal possessions he had managed to bring out of Sedan was the first draft of a work which he had originally been naïve enough to think might be printed in the *Mercure galant*, a Parisian monthly whose editor (and, in the manner of the times, sole contributor) often published letters from readers. Bayle pretended to be writing as a Catholic, but he was aware that no censor would be taken in by this, and when he belatedly realised that the periodical was subject to royal censorship, he gave up the idea of sending it his piece. In Rotterdam, he took it up again, adding to the text, but still maintaining the fiction of Catholic authorship. The *Letter on the Comet** appeared anonymously (this was standard practice) in March 1682, published by Leers at Rotterdam. It was well received, and Bayle revised and further enlarged it for a second edition, with the definitive title of *Miscellaneous Reflections on the Comet*, in September 1683. The comet in question was the one that had been sighted over western Europe in December 1680 – without, however, causing the panic fear among the masses that the sudden appearance of such phenomena had usually done. The letter form in which the work appeared was a literary convention which Bayle

---

* For the French titles of Bayle's works, see 'Further reading', p. 92 below.

found particularly attractive, as it gave him the chance to write in a lively, informal manner and to indulge a natural taste for digression, in a way that would not have been tolerated in a formal treatise. The *Letter* was addressed to a Doctor of the Sorbonne, that is to say, to a Catholic theologian. On the surface, it is the work of a partisan of Cartesian mechanism who demonstrates at length that the presence of a comet in the heavens cannot conceivably result in harmful physical occurrences on earth. To those who asserted that such conjunctions were a fact of experience, Bayle retorted that 'given the way things normally happen, it is just as likely that, after any year you care to name, there will be a major catastrophe somewhere or other in the world, as it is that an inhabitant of Paris will see someone passing by in the street when he looks out over the Pont Saint-Michel' (*Misc. Refl.* xxiii). But the heart of the work, and its real originality, is to be found in the theological arguments Bayle adduces for denying that comets have supernatural significance. It is wrong to contend that God has miraculously conjured up comets as warnings to mankind to repent and return to the paths of piety. If this were so, he would be stimulating the zeal of idolators, for piety, to the majority of men, means idolatry. (This may seem a perfidious remark, but it is not. Unlike the average observer whose horizons were confined to Europe, Bayle was able, as a member of a religious minority, to conceive of Christianity itself as a minority religion in the context of the world as a whole.) Now the true God abhors nothing more than he does idolatry (not even atheism, as we shall see). Moreover, the true God is the Father of the whole of mankind, and is not concerned with only a part of it. It follows that, for the theologian, the unexpected appearance of a comet can have no supernatural significance. Rather, Bayle claims, it must obey astronomical laws as yet undiscovered. Halley would begin to elucidate these laws not long after Bayle's work was written.

This first published work of Bayle's is also, in a disguised and somewhat muted way, a work of Protestant controversy. Although on the face of it he is pouring scorn on the idolatrous practices of the pagans of classical antiquity, there is little doubt that his biting attack on superstition is aimed at the Church of Rome. This aspect of the work naturally amused and delighted the refugees, but the *Miscellaneous Reflections* also found favour in France. It pleased the many partisans of Cartesian mechanism, Gallicans to whom popular piety on the Spanish or Italian model was anathema, and educated people who appreciated Bayle's relaxed, teasing style as bearing what Boileau was to pronounce to be the hallmark of good writing.

If the refugee communities thought well of the anonymous author of the *Miscellaneous Reflections*, they were positively enthusiastic about the unknown controversialist who in 1682 published at 'Villefranche' (actually Amsterdam), under the imprint of 'Pierre Le Blanc' (in fact Wolfgang), the *General Criticism of Monsieur Maimbourg's History of Calvinism*. A second edition followed in November, and in March 1683 the work was accorded the supreme accolade of being burned by the public hangman in Paris, which naturally brought it enormous publicity and greatly increased its potential readership. The *General Criticism* was written in a fortnight, without revision and, once again, in the form of letters to a friend. By its derisively courteous tone as well as its arguments, it inaugurated a new style of controversy. Maimbourg was a successful author of popular histories, and an ex-Jesuit whose persistent gallicanism had cost him expulsion from his Society but had been duly rewarded by the French court; his book venomously attacked all Huguenots, past and present alike, as troublemakers and subversives who had been responsible for all the ills of the Wars of Religion and still constituted a dangerous residue which had to be brought back into line by force. On the face of it, it was absurd, at this time, to depict the Huguenots as a threat to the safety of the realm, when they were in fact a minority which had already suffered to the point that even everyday living had become intolerably difficult for them. However, it was astute of Maimbourg to represent them as even a potential danger to an ideal of public order which had only recently become a reality in France, and which therefore seemed a precious and fragile possession that all Frenchmen must treasure: to remind them of the fearful anarchy of the second half of the sixteenth century and the troubled early years of the reign of Louis XIII was a highly effective controversial tactic. The standard Protestant reply to such imputations was generally ineffectual, consisting as it did in discussing, point by point, what was said about the Wars of Religion in the light of equally biased testimony from the opposite side which showed the Protestants as victims instead of aggressors, and in blackening the character of their enemies, the House of Guise and the League.

Bayle did not completely abandon this approach. Above all, though, he adopted an entirely new method, which consisted in underlining the lack of certainty that must result from so many convinced but contradictory testimonies. A reasonable man, he argues, cannot afford to trust biased witnesses. Instead, in conformity with Cartesian principles, which Bayle here adapts to history, he must suspend judgement, and accept as established facts only those for which there is independent confirmation, or on which all witnesses agree:

occasionally, we can claim to have established historical truth right down to points of detail. For example, it is possible to be convinced of the truth of a fact, or a project, or a particular motive, when everyone agrees about it; or when, even though it is discreditable to one party, that party nevertheless admits it; or when it does credit to one party, and the other party does not seek to contradict it. (*Gen. Crit.* II i)

It is possible to know, *grosso modo*, how things have happened – what battles were fought, or what treaties were signed – but for the most part it is impossible to know enough to be able to evaluate the responsibility of those concerned. The *General Criticism* postulated criteria for historical objectivity and, where they were lacking, advocated what some have criticised as being Bayle's 'historical pyrrhonism', in other words scepticism taken to extremes. In reality, it was the way history was treated as a literary genre that Bayle rejected: he wanted it to become a scientific discipline, dominated by an ideal of scrupulous impartiality and based on a rigorous critique of sources.

There were plenty of Catholics in France who were hostile to the Jesuits, and were not displeased to see the *General Criticism* dispose so effectively of Maimbourg's malevolent arguments. With the Refuge the book had an outstanding success, and it was this which stimulated attempts to discover the identity of its author, something that Bayle, well aware of the harm to his family that could result, had been at pains to conceal. Unfortunately his anonymity was breached, and word of his authorship reached the French Embassy, with disastrous consequences, as we shall see.

In March 1684, encouraged by earlier successes, Bayle began to edit a monthly, the *News of the Republic of Letters*, printed at Amsterdam, in which he analysed a dozen recently published books in detail. His reviews, which were extremely well informed, were written in the same affable and engaging way that had already won him so many readers. Although the new periodical did not make him any money, it brought him a supply of new books and, above all, correspondents. Postal rates in the seventeenth century were very heavy and charged to the recipient, but all Bayle's were paid by his publisher, Desbordes. Thus his venture into journalism gave him the chance to be at the centre of a network of correspondents, a luxury he could never have afforded out of his modest salary as a professor at the École Illustre. The *News* was Bayle's third great literary success. The periodical answered a need and filled a gap. Authors and enquirers took the initiative in sending him material from all the parts of Europe to which the Huguenots had begun to disperse even before the Revocation. The *News* was well received in France. Although thanks to the vigilant censorship it soon became more difficult (and so more expensive) to import copies, they were distributed none the less and many readers wrote to Bayle or sent him books. But the refugees on their own were in any case a large enough public to ensure the viability of a publication which was so successful that it inspired the founding of rival journals. As more anti-Protestant books were published in France, and provoked replies from the Refuge, the *News* acquired a more militant character, though works of erudition, medical observations and scientific discussions were still reviewed. At the same time, Bayle's tone remained urbane, even after the Revocation, although he did allow himself, when writing about French religious policy, the luxury of 'a little rhetorical figure called Irony' (*NRL* Feb. 1686, vii).

In March 1685 appeared the *New Letters by the Author of the General Criticism*. This met with nothing like the success of its predecessor. Bayle's coolly objective discussion of various episodes of the Wars of Religion seemed incongruous at a time when the authorities at Versailles were battering the French Reformed Churches into extinction, and his ideas on civil toleration either passed over his readers' heads or else accorded ill with their own partisan fervour.

Bayle's mother had died, probably of tuberculosis, in 1675, and in the spring of 1684 Joseph, who was tutor to a Protestant family in Paris, had been carried off in a few days by an infectious disease. In March 1685, Jean Bayle died. But the worst was still to come. On 10 June 1685 Pierre's brother Jacob was arrested, and from enquiries in Paris it was clear that it was because they could not get their hands on the author of the *General Criticism* himself that the authorities had seized his nearest relative. After being kept captive for five months in an unhealthy cell, where he was visited daily by a Jesuit priest who offered to have him released if he would abjure, the young pastor finally succumbed to the appalling conditions and died in prison on 12 November 1685. When the news eventually reached Rotterdam, Bayle suffered the worst blow of his life, especially since he knew his own failure to conceal his identity as the author of the *General Criticism* was indirectly the cause of his brother's death.

The agony which Pierre experienced as a result of Jacob's death completely undermined his faith in divine Providence. From now on, as we shall see, he found it impossible to accept any of the soothing pseudo-solutions to the problem, or the mystery, of Evil that traditional theology offered. At the same time, his hatred of religious intolerance could only be strengthened and deepened by the actual examples by which he was surrounded. Refugees were flooding into the United Provinces in ever-increasing numbers, many with stories of every kind of atrocity, and after the Revocation (22 October 1685) they were joined by the exiled pastors in their hundreds, including

Basnage. Unlike a layman, a pastor could choose between abjuration and exile, but if he chose exile, he had to leave behind him not only his goods, but any children who were more than seven years old, to be brought up as Catholics.

After his brother's death, Bayle put all his energies into writing. Although editing the *News of the Republic of Letters* was in itself almost a full-time occupation, Bayle also managed to write books. The first to appear, in March 1686, was a pamphlet of exemplary vigour entitled *The True State of Wholly Catholic France in the Reign of Louis XIV*. From a literary point of view, it was the best thing Bayle ever wrote. As before, it was cast in the form of an exchange of letters. A Catholic abbé writes to a 'reasonable' refugee, whom he asks to comment on a letter from an outraged Protestant, hoping that the refugee will be provoked into condemning the excesses of his co-religionist. Not for the first time, Bayle presents widely divergent points of view in an even-handed way, and leaves it to the reader to draw the necessary conclusions. The letter of outrage, it is true, does give eloquent expression to a bitter desire for vengeance that Bayle himself must have felt, but equally representative of the author is the figure of the 'reasonable' refugee, who tries to avoid the pitfalls of sectarianism.

Simultaneously, Bayle started work on a lengthy treatise on religious toleration, the *Philosophical Commentary*, to which we shall return. But in February 1687, suffering from a combination of depression and overwork, he stopped editing the *News of the Republic of Letters*, gave up his teaching and took several months' enforced rest.

When he arrived in Rotterdam at the age of thirty-four, Bayle was certainly a Calvinist. He may not have been a fervent one (and sentimental effusions are in any case not much associated with the French seventeenth century) but he was a convinced and practising one, and he continued to practise his religion until the day he died. Many critics have taxed him with flagrant hypocrisy and claimed that eventually he stopped believing altogether. But it is equally likely that his beliefs were, and remained, heterodox. The spiritual crisis brought about by Jacob Bayle's death for his faith, and by the trauma of the

Revocation, had the decisive effect of concentrating Bayle's attention on the problem of evil and the question of religious toleration. Inevitably, more traditional Calvinist concerns were pushed into the background. Of course, many other refugees experienced a crisis of this kind (if not of this precise nature). The problems Bayle set himself to solve were common to the whole Refuge, but it was Bayle's distinction to pose them with exemplary clarity and to reject ready-made answers. To stress how directly even Bayle's theoretical notions sprang from his personal experience is not to underrate his intellectual originality, but, on the contrary, to emphasise it. Where toleration was concerned, two decades had not passed before his personal solution had been adopted at least partly, by most of the Refuge, to be followed soon after by the whole of European Protestantism.

Toleration (1687–93)

After a long absence, Bayle went back to the École Illustre, but not to the *News of the Republic of Letters*, which he was happy to leave in other hands, particularly since in September 1687 Henri Basnage de Beauval, the younger brother of his old friend, after escaping from France, had begun to publish a periodical called *History of the Works of the Learned* (*Histoire des ouvrages des savants*). As well as giving him the benefit of his considerable experience as an editor, Bayle transferred to him his own network of correspondents. Still endeavouring to remain anonymous, he managed to complete and publish the successive volumes of his *Philosophical Commentary*, or to give it its full title, *Philosophical Commentary on the words of Our Lord 'Compel them to come in', in which it is proved by demonstrative reasoning that nothing is more abominable than to make conversions by force, and in which all the sophistry of those who would do so is refuted, likewise the apologia made by St Augustine for persecution*. Volumes I and II had appeared in October 1686. Volume III came out in June 1687, and a supplement at the very beginning of 1688. The work, ostensibly 'translated from the English of Mr. John Fox of Bruggs', developed more systematically some of the ideas on the 'erring conscience' already adumbrated in the *New Letters by the Author of the General Criticism*, so that knowledgeable readers had no difficulty in identifying Bayle as its imaginary English author, and a Dutch printer (it was brought out by Wolfgang of Amsterdam) as its supposed publisher at Canterbury and Hamburg.

Bayle's only point in taking such precautions seems to have been to avoid open conflict with Jurieu, who, though he attacked the work, also pretended not to know who had written it. Although formally Jurieu remained on good terms with Bayle, their relationship cooled off rapidly. Like so many pastors of his generation, Jurieu stayed faithful to the authoritarian dogmatism of traditional Calvinism, and to the Augustinian strain in Christian theology, according to which persecution was only illicit if undertaken on behalf of a 'false' belief. In taking this view, Jurieu did not differ in principle from the French Catholic clergy, and when he denounced the latter it was not for their intolerance but because they were attacking the form of Christianity which he believed to be the purest and the best. For the same reason, he thoroughly approved the discriminatory measures taken against Catholics in England and criticised James II for relaxing them. There are parallels for this kind of mentality in our own day, when there are still people who believe that 'truth' has the right to take oppressive measures which 'error' has not, although nowadays, of course, 'truth' is usually political rather than religious. Dogmatism of any kind not only inevitably leads to such conclusions, but often goes hand in hand, as it did in Jurieu's case, with a burning faith. The fact that Bayle eschewed dogmatism has done much to make him appear an unbeliever, but it is surely his own portrait that he painted when describing Melanchthon in the *Dictionary*:

> he was naturally good-natured and pacific, possessed great intelligence, had read widely, and knew a vast amount. These characteristics, when found together, usually make men indecisive. A man of great intellectual capacity, backed up by extensive knowledge, rarely finds that all the wrongs are on the same side: rather, he finds strong and weak points in each party. (*Dict.* Melanchthon n. I)

The *Philosophical Commentary* did indeed call for scrupulous respect for the conscience of each individual, even if he were 'in error', or in other words a follower of a 'false' religion; for, as Bayle puts it, God

> has laid upon us a burden proportionate to our strength, which is to seek truth until, after having searched sincerely, we believe we have found it; to love the truth that we have found; and to regulate our lives according to its principles, however great their demands may be. In other words, conscience is given to us to be the touchstone of that truth which we are commanded to obey and to love. (*Phil. Comm.* ɪɪ x)

Hence 'even if the person persecuted is worthless, the persecutor is always unjust' (ibid. ɪɪɪ x). 'It is not a matter of what you force people to do, but that you are wrong to use force at all ... as soon as you do so, you commit a most wicked act, categorically opposed to the spirit of any religion and, above all, to that of the Gospel' (ibid. ɪ xvii).

Jurieu, blinded by the fervour of a militant, could only see an apology for indifferentism in this argument. Nor was it only, or above all, on theoretical grounds that he rejected Bayle's thesis. There were immediate tactical reasons for Jurieu, in the twice-monthly *Pastoral Letters* (*Lettres pastorales adressées aux fidèles de France*) which he addressed not only to the Refuge but by clandestine routes to the Huguenots who were still in France, to indulge in frantic excoriation of Catholicism. His aim was to discourage those who had been forced to become 'New Catholics' from actually practising the religion they had been made to adopt. Moreover, on the basis of his own interpretation of the Book of Revelation together with reports of mystical happenings amongst the oppressed Protestants in various parts of southern France, Jurieu prophesied that the whole situation was about to be spectacularly reversed. Nothing therefore could have seemed worse-timed to him than Bayle's plea to respect all religious convictions. It was something which the Catholics were sure to take advantage of. The ·*Philosophical Commentary* taught that each person should tolerate the other man's religion. Tendentiously interpreted, it could be taken to imply that

Protestants should not only tolerate Catholicism but cease to oppose it in principle. There have been hawks and doves at various times in history. Bayle appeared to favour disarmament just at the moment when, in Jurieu's eyes, the need was to galvanise Protestants everywhere into action, in view of the new European war which was bound to begin at any minute. It would be a Holy War, a Crusade, in which God would be sure to give the victory to those who had already put their trust in Him.

Jurieu's extravagant ideas show how deep were the wounds the Revocation inflicted on the Huguenots, and for that reason they deserve better than mockery. In fairness, we should say no more than that prophecies about the immediate future are always hazardous, particularly where the personal intervention of divine Providence is involved. As for Bayle himself, his brother's death had taught him, once and for all, that so far as human beings can tell, virtue is not 'rewarded' in this life, and that those who lose their battles, although defamed by history, are not necessarily those whose cause is wrong. Anyone whose nose had been rubbed in the dirt by events would have found this a reasonable enough proposition. Yet many refugees, encouraged by Jurieu, were so childishly confident in divine protection that they convinced themselves that in the very near future things would change radically and that they would be able to return to their native country with their heads held high. The total, and to a large extent unforeseen, success of William of Orange's expedition to England in 1688 seemed to lend colour to their optimism. Jurieu saw the finger of God himself in the way things had happened, and greeted as an authentic miracle the 'Protestant wind' which had come to the aid of the Dutch fleet as it lay becalmed at Torbay.

Jurieu also tried to provide a theoretical justification for William's actions, and this led him to abandon divine right absolutism and to revive the ideas of the sixteenth-century monarchomachists who had postulated a tacit contract between kings and their subjects, giving the latter the right of resistance to a monarch who exceeded his own rights and behaved like a tyrant. This was a way both of justifying the English for having deprived James II of his throne, and of inciting the refugees to take up the fight against Louis XIV. Jurieu was, it is true, prudent enough to preach only passive disobedience to the Huguenots still living in France, and then only where religion was at stake; but his diatribes were bound to increase the hostility of the French authorities towards a section of the population that was already suspected of holding disloyal opinions.

Bayle was increasingly angered by Jurieu's attitude. It was hypocritical, indecent and dishonest, he felt, to interpret the designs of Providence in such a way as to justify whoever happened to have the upper hand for the time being. Moreover, he maintained his own support for the divine right theory to the extent of holding William III's accession to the English throne to be tainted with immorality, because the son-in-law had driven out the father-in-law. Above all, it seemed to him that in the short term there was only one political strategy which might conceivably encourage the French authorities to re-establish the Edict of Nantes, and that was for the refugees to keep unswervingly to their original political line. Once they were seen at Versailles as factious elements with subversive ('republican') ideas about the cases in which it was right to offer resistance to kings, they would forfeit all hope of being allowed to return home on political grounds, even if the fact of their heresy were to be passed over; by the same token, their brethren in France would be considered contaminated by their dangerous views, and would be bound to suffer even greater hardships.

There was now total opposition between Bayle and Jurieu on every issue, whether concerning abstract theory or the tactics which would best serve the Huguenot cause in the circumstances of the moment. Jurieu was appalled by Bayle's defence of toleration, while Bayle was exasperated by Jurieu's call for the refugees to take part in a Holy War under the banner of William of Orange. The break-up of their relationship was inevitable and, when it came, traumatic.

At the beginning of 1689, another anonymous work in the form of fictitious letters appeared, the short *Reply of a New Convert to the letters of a Refugee*, in which a former Huguenot who had gone over to Catholicism was represented as being scandalised by pamphlets emanating from the Refuge that contradicted traditional Calvinist political theory. Taking a step further, Bayle brought out in April 1690 an *Important Warning to the Refugees concerning their Impending Return to France*. Bayle's denials that he had written the work were casuistical rather than categorical. The original idea for the book seems, it is true, to have come from Daniel de Larroque, a refugee pastor who eventually found the political climate of the Refuge so oppressive that he abjured and returned to France, but the final text of the *Warning*, which was a much amplified version of Larroque's presumed first sketch, is certainly from Bayle's own pen. Claiming to be written by a Catholic, the pamphlet is a biting attack on the apostasy of the Refuge in matters of political theory, and a mocking commentary on the Protestant propagandists' presentation of recent events. Bayle probably expected that by adopting an aggressive manner he would provoke denials from at least some members of the Refuge, and that other voices as well as his own would thus proclaim the continued loyalty of at least a section of the Huguenots to the theory of divine right. If so, he was sadly mistaken, for the replies to the *Warning* continued to be full of nothing but panegyrics of William of Orange, arguments in defence of the English Revolution and affirmations of the right of popular resistance.

Jurieu, who was ill at the time the book came out, did not at first suspect that his former friend was the author, and it was not until April 1691 that he voiced his unbridled anger in his *Examination of a pamphlet ... (Examen d'un libelle ...)*, in which he accused Bayle of treachery and virtually asked the Dutch authorities for his head. Happily for Bayle, Jurieu ruined his own case by raising the spectre of a wholly imaginary conspiracy. His extravagant accusations had, for the moment at least, no effect on the traditionally liberal and unexcitable Dutch rulers. Meanwhile, in alliance with Basnage de Beauval whom Jurieu had also vilified, Bayle launched into an unsavoury war of pamphlets in which both sides descended to base personal attacks. Some months later, in May 1692, when he had recovered his equilibrium, Bayle published, in the form of a letter to a friend, his *Project for a critical dictionary*, in which he showed that he had returned to his labours as a scholar. But in October 1693 Jurieu's attacks eventually bore fruit. Owing to a change in the political complexion of the Rotterdam municipal council, Bayle's post at the École Illustre was suppressed. He found compensation in the fact that Leers, his friend and publisher, undertook to make him a small annuity pending the publication of the *Dictionary*. This meant that Bayle could now devote himself entirely to what he described as 'the most delightful pursuit any man of letters could hope for' (Preface to the first edition of the *Dictionary*).

When the polemics with Jurieu began, in 1691, Bayle and his supporters were apparently at a disadvantage. Jurieu dominated the biannual meetings of the Walloon synods, and had persuaded them to censure various 'tolerant' pastors. But he could not damage Bayle and Basnage de Beauval directly, because they were laymen; they were also persuasive writers and often had their readers laughing with them at their adversary. Above all, Jurieu had attacked too many people, propounded too many unconsidered theological notions and mixed politics and religion in too cavalier a way for his enormous prestige amongst the refugees to remain untarnished. Nor was there any sign that the miraculous events he had predicted were actually taking place. Moreover, religious toleration, against which Jurieu had set his face, was a logical idea for victims of persecution to espouse, and it continued to gain ground, notably amongst the younger refugees. The Refuge was in the process of losing touch with the characteristic assumptions of the French classical age, and was turning towards the diametrically opposed ideas of Locke. Not that Locke's influence was direct. It was through Jurieu that the Refuge came to the contract theory of society and the notion of the rights of the people, and through Bayle that they embraced the idea of religious toleration. Paradoxically, the outlook of a whole section of the common readership of these two bitter enemies was formed through a combination of the favourite ideas of each of them.

The Dictionary

The *Historical and Critical Dictionary*, first published in three folio volumes in December 1696, was the only work by Bayle to bear the author's name. It is a huge arsenal of scholarship based on prodigious reading and on the compilation of numerous dossiers of notes (nobody worked from file-cards in the seventeenth century). Although it was almost impossible for it to be distributed in France, it sold extremely well in the northern and Protestant parts of Europe, despite its high price, and it made a handsome profit for its publisher. It is a bio-bibliographical dictionary, dealing with people rather than places, the subjects being figures from history and, for the most part, writers and thinkers. There are articles on Old Testament and classical figures, but what we now call the Middle Ages is only thinly represented. The modern period takes up a good deal of space, with Italian humanists, figures from French history beginning with the time of the Wars of Religion, Protestant theologians in large numbers and from several countries, and recent philosophers such as Hobbes and Spinoza.

The preface underlines the aims already stated in the *Project*, and describes the work's genesis and structure. A quarter of a century earlier, a Catholic priest from Lyons by the name of Moréri had compiled a *Historical Dictionary* which evidently filled a gap, for it had been reprinted several times, with additional material, in both France and Holland. In adding the word 'critical' to his own title, Bayle makes immediately clear the difference between his work and Moréri's, which he is ostensibly only augmenting and revising by inserting new articles and expanding others. It is true that the reason Bayle has no article on Plato is that he was satisfied with Moréri's. But elsewhere he makes an enormous number of corrections and, although his own lack of knowledge of Germanic languages restricted him to works written in Latin, he also corrects the Catholic bias of Moréri's *Dictionary* by the inclusion of much Protestant material.

The *Dictionary* owed the favourable reception which immediately greeted it to the accurate, clear and often recondite information which it conveyed in so convenient a form. Its continuing fame and its lasting appeal have another source. The text of the articles is made up of concise biographies in a rather impersonal style, but it is in the footnotes, often many times longer than the text, that Bayle gives full rein to his taste for digression and displays his own personality, in the same spontaneous and witty way as he does in his letters. As well as ridiculing adversaries such as Jurieu, Bayle uses the notes to expound his own ideas on theology, metaphysics, ethics and politics. The *Dictionary* becomes a weapon in a war against religious intolerance on the one hand, and an outline of the history of philosophy on the other. It includes a methodical demolition of traditional theodicies (or attempts to explain the presence of evil in God's Creation), furnishes an arsenal of anticlerical arguments – the clergy having always been the chief agents of religious persecution – and is seasoned with a mixture of bizarre, colourful and sometimes salty anecdotes. To read these brilliant and often original miniature essays, spiced with wit as well as rigorously argued, is to be aware of the delight Bayle himself must have taken in writing them.

At the same time, such an enormous undertaking was obviously burdensome. Leers put each article into the press as Bayle completed it. Bayle was correcting the proofs of one article while writing another, and could only get ahead of the printer in the depths of winter, when the cold was so intense that the printer's ink froze and he had to shut down the presses. This accounts for the fact that the same questions recur, sometimes unexpectedly, at different points in the work, and explains why Bayle had sometimes to insert an idea or a piece of information much later than its logical place in the alphabet, the relevant sheets having already been printed. We should not confuse Bayle's situation with that of Diderot when the latter was editing the *Encyclopaedia*. The reason Diderot held back certain references was to put the censor off the track, whereas in Holland there was no censorship. Leers's workmen did him proud and the three volumes are a magnificent example of the typographer's art. The text of each article runs across the head of the page; the notes are disposed in two columns at the foot, each keyed to the text by a letter of the alphabet; the margins carry references, running into thousands, hardly a single one of which is inaccurate – an astonishing testimony to Bayle's erudition.

The first edition sold out so rapidly that Bayle immediately began work on a second, with additional articles and notes. Jurieu had been mocked in various places in the work, and this did not diminish his animosity towards the author. On his initiative, the Walloon Consistory in Rotterdam summoned Bayle to explain certain things that threatened to scandalise the faithful. The author was accused of gratuitous obscenity, of showing favour to atheists, pyrrhonians (or sceptics) and Manicheans (heretics who believed that power over the world was equally divided between God and Satan); and, finally, of failing to show respect for the sacred memory of King David. This caused Bayle to add four *Clarifications* to the second edition, published in December 1701. These are extremely valuable for any assessment of Bayle's true outlook. He also cut out the offending passages from the article 'David', but this gave rise to so many protests from intending purchasers that Leers then reprinted the complete text of the first edition as an appendix. Although Leers took full responsibility for his action, Bayle was doubtless aware of what was happening. His somewhat equivocal attitude to the Bible is, as we shall see, one of the most controversial aspects of his thought.

The final years (1702–6)

The *Dictionary* made other enemies, including some who were as hostile to Jurieu as Bayle was. A rationalistic theology close in spirit to English latitudinarianism had been gradually taking root in the Refuge. Its origins were various. One source was Arminianism. The Arminians, also known as Remonstrants, had objected to some of the mòst rigid tenets of Calvinism, notably predestination, much earlier in the seventeenth century. Their liberal attitude had failed to carry the day at the Synod of Dordrecht (1618–19), and led to a schism in the Dutch Church. Another source was the theological orientation of the Reformed Academy of Saumur in France, which had tried to mitigate the decisions taken at Dordrecht, and had won the support of a

large number of French pastors. More generally, there was the
influence of Cartesianism with its reliance on self-evidence as
the criterion of truth. Jurieu, in particular, had tried to discredit
the adherents of this outlook by labelling them 'socinians'. This
was an attempt to identify them with the ultra-rationalistic and
anti-trinitarian form of Protestantism inspired by the Italians
Lelio Sozzini and his nephew Fausto which had flourished in
Poland for many years at the end of the sixteenth century and
during the early part of the seventeenth. These were all currents
of thought that were to contribute to the rise of eighteenth-
century deism, but the 'rationalists' who attacked Bayle were
still a long way from that point. All they wanted to do was to
establish that the conclusions reached by reason and the articles
of the Christian faith did not contradict one another. Like the
English latitudinarians or Low Church liberals who professed a
'reasonable' and 'enlightened' form of Christianity, they were
complacent optimists as well as being enthusiastic partisans of
toleration. They thought that they had Bayle as an ally in their
defence of toleration, and reacted with bitterness when they
discovered, on the appearance of the *Dictionary*, that they and
he had little more in common than an antipathy for intolerance.

It is or course true that Bayle never tires of emphasising the
total disparity he believes there to be between the demands of
human reason and the content of the Christian revelation. He
takes the view, however, that this disparity will only be found
upsetting by someone who overvalues the scope of reason.
Properly speaking, reason is an essentially critical faculty, which
can do no more than establish separate zones of coherence
(notably in matters of ethics), but can never give rise to total
explanations or grasp the basis of reality.

A true believer, who has correctly understood the spirit of his
religion, does not expect that it will be capable of refuting, by
reason alone, the difficulties raised by reason. He knows that
natural things are in no way proportional to supernatural
things. ... One must necessarily choose between philosophy
and the Gospel: if you want to believe only what is clear and

distinct, choose philosophy and abandon Christianity, but if you want to believe the incomprehensible mysteries of religion, choose Christianity and abandon philosophy, for to grasp both the clear and distinct and the incomprehensible at the same time is impossible ... A true Christian will only laugh at the subtleties of the philosophers ... Faith will raise him above the regions where the storms of disputation rage. (*Dict.* Third Clarification, iv)

The rationalists took offence at Bayle's root and branch criticism of their facile metaphysics, with its pretensions to reconcile reason and faith, earthly happiness and virtue, and to solve the enigma of Evil with rhetorical platitudes. The bitter pessimism of the *Dictionary*, which depicts man as being as wicked as he is wretched, exasperated them almost as much as the mocking refutation of exorbitant claims on behalf of human reason. Authors now long and deservedly forgotten vied with one another in attempting to refute Bayle's ideas. In the vocabulary of modern politics, Bayle was under attack simultaneously from Jurieu on the right and the rationalists on the left. He seemed like a lone figure whom it was impossible to classify, like his own *Dictionary*, which the French accused of being anti-Catholic while Jurieu found it scandalously pro-Roman – a conflict of opinion which Bayle himself no doubt saw as proof of his having achieved the impartiality he had been aiming at.

What Bayle could not incorporate into the *Dictionary* in the way of erudition and scholarly discussion, he utilised in the last works he wrote, which were answers to the philosophical and theological objections of his rationalist opponents. The *Continuation of the Miscellaneous Reflections*, published in August 1704, took up again some of the topics of the *Miscellaneous Reflections on the Comet* of a quarter of a century earlier. Among other things, Bayle refutes those authors who find proof of the existence of God in humanity's alleged consensus on the matter. The most commonly held views, he argues, are often the most fallacious. 'If the general agreement that God exists is a good means of proving that He exists, then the general agreement that there is a plurality of gods would be a good proof of the existence of several divinities' (*Continuation*, xxviii). (Bayle is referring here to the erstwhile popularity of polytheism, which could be said to have enjoyed universal consent in times past.)

The *Reply to the Questions of a Provincial*, in letter form like the previous work, harks back to the days when Bayle himself was a provincial filled with curiosity about the rich intellectual life of far-off centres of learning. It enabled him, among other things, to reply to the attacks of the least obscure of the rationalists, the Arminian theologian Jean Le Clerc (1651–1736). Le Clerc had put forward a thoroughly orthodox explanation of evil as being the result of man's abuse of his privileged gift of free will. The *Reply* covers four volumes, the first of which appeared in October 1703, while the fourth was published posthumously in February 1707. At the same time appeared the unfinished *Conversations of Maxime and Thémiste* which Bayle had written against Le Clerc and the pastor Isaac Jaquelot in the last few weeks of his life. Although this work is not without a hint of bitterness, Bayle seems to have found relief from his last illness in writing it.

Meanwhile, during the autumn of 1706, Jurieu had published the last and best of his attacks on Bayle, a work entitled *The Philosopher of Rotterdam Accused, Charged and Convicted* (*Le Philosophe de Rotterdam accusé, atteint et convaincu*). Bayle is probably to be believed when he says that he never deigned to read Jurieu's pamphlet. Knowing that the kind of punctilious orthodoxy of which Jurieu was the self-appointed champion was rapidly losing its hold, and that the cause of toleration was virtually won, he reserved his fire for the rationalists.

Very few copies of the two editions of the *Dictionary* found their way into France. It was not put on sale there until the death of Louis XIV in 1715, though from 1720 onwards it was to have a large readership. The publication of such a monumental work of scholarship nevertheless established Bayle's reputation and gave it a European dimension. Bayle had not taken the advice of refugee friends who wanted him to dedicate the work to the English Secretary of State Sir William Trumbull (1639–1716). Apart from the store he set by independence, he argued that he had too often been ironical about self-interested flattery to indulge in it himself. However he did go in 1700 with Basnage to The Hague to meet, at their request, Sophie, Dowager Electress of Hanover, and her daughter, the Electress of Brandenburg and future Queen of Prussia, though his thick southern accent made what little he said incomprehensible to these great ladies.

In 1698, Bayle had become friendly with Anthony Ashley Cooper (to become, in November 1699, the third Earl of Shaftesbury), whom he saw often during the latter's frequent long stays in Rotterdam. Bayle had probably been introduced to him by an old friend, the Quaker Benjamin Furly, who had settled in Rotterdam and through whom he had already met John Locke and the historian Gilbert Burnet – later a bishop. How close the friendship with Shaftesbury was, despite the difference in social standing, can be seen from the fact that the nobleman managed to persuade the punctilious Bayle to accept gifts of books and even a watch, a luxury which the author of the *Dictionary* would normally have scorned. Shaftesbury also had a protégé in London, a young refugee called Pierre Des Maizeaux, who admired Bayle and kept him informed about intellectual life in England: later, he was to be Bayle's first biographer and the English translator of his writings.

During the last years of his life, Bayle became a kind of tourist attraction. He greeted his visitors affably and with a loquacity unheard-of in his younger days. He assured the abbé de Polignac that he was 'a good Protestant' since he was in the habit of protesting 'against everything anyone says or does'. This is the kind of joke old men make, and Bayle had indeed thought of himself as an old man for many years, acquiring in the process, he told one of his correspondents, a 'philosophical indifference' to his own eventual fate (letter to his cousin Naudis, 3 Feb. 1700, *OD*^{2} I B, 188a).

Throughout his stay in Holland, Bayle had caught a cold every winter, which lasted, with spells of coughing, until the spring. Friends had told him about 'Locke's principle that it is bad for one's health to cover up one's head' (letter to Coste, 15 May 1702, *OD*^{2} IV 820a), but he did not dare leave off the wig he always wore. In the spring of 1705 the cough did not go away, and tuberculosis set in. Bayle, who had no desire to prolong 'an ailing life' which he had always held to be 'worse than death' (as he says in letters written in October 1706), refused the bizarre remedies recommended by his friends. During the last few months of his life, when talking aggravated his coughing fits, he saw no visitors. When he died, probably as the result of a heart attack, on 28 December 1706, he was alone and in bed, but surrounded by books and papers. In accordance with his last wishes, he was buried in the common grave of the Walloon Church at Rotterdam. He bequeathed his supplementary notes to the *Dictionary* to his friend and publisher Leers. He had little capital to leave, having invested most of his money in annuities for himself and his niece, Jacob Bayle's daughter, whose death occurred only shortly before his own. He left some of his books to his executor, Jacques Basnage, and instructed him to distribute the rest to friends, as well as to send what little money there was, along with his personal papers, to cousins in France. Basnage carried out these instructions once the War of the Spanish Succession was over, and Bayle's papers found their way into the hands of a distant cousin, who promptly lost the greater part of them.

A few hours before he died, Bayle had written in a letter to his friend Pastor Terson, 'I die a Christian philosopher, convinced of and filled with God's goodness and mercy' (D'Argens, *Secret Memoirs of the Republic of Letters* (*Mémoires secrets de la république des lettres*), 1738, p. 1068). The words 'I die a philosopher' had been uttered by the notorious unbeliever Averroes, the twelfth-century Muslim philosopher who was in his time the most celebrated commentator on Aristotle. In his article on Averroes in the *Dictionary*, Bayle had recalled (note H) that in the Bible Balaam had expressed the wish to die 'the death of the just' (Num. 23:10). But Bayle did add the word 'Christian', and however laconic, his own profession of faith was still a profession of religious faith.

Five years later, the *Dictionary* was translated into English. Fifteen years later it began to be read throughout France, so widely that, as statistics show, it eventually became the work most often found in eighteenth-century private libraries. And less than twenty-five years after Bayle's death, the publication of four folio volumes of *Miscellaneous Works* made, in conjunction with the *Dictionary*, every one of his writings readily accessible to anyone interested in reading them. The posthumous career of one of the Fathers of the Enlightenment had begun.

3 Bayle's basic presuppositions

A tincture of Cartesianism

Like everyone of his generation in France, Bayle was influenced by Descartes (1596–1650). Descartes had made a clean break with the two most powerful philosophical influences of the day, Aristotelian logic and the empiricism of the schoolmen, who held that 'there is nothing in the intellect that does not have its origin in the sense'. For Descartes, all truth is deducible from, and has the same characteristics of clearness and distinctness, as the primary intuition 'I think, therefore I am'. Descartes also laid the foundations for a complete system of mechanistic physics. However, until he read the works of Malebranche, Bayle was not a close student of Descartes's philosophy, which he knew only through second-rate popularisations.

Malebranche (1638–1715) was a priest of the Oratory, and a fervent admirer of Descartes, from whom he gained the inspiration for his own brand of rationalism. He elaborated a personal, highly original metaphysics which can be described as a kind of Christian Platonism. Bayle was never very clear in his own mind as to the essential differences between the philosophies of Descartes and Malebranche, and although he thought of himself as a Cartesian it would be more accurate to speak of him as a Malebranchist. In any case, the theory of knowledge in its most abstract form did not really interest him, while his ignorance of mathematics prevented him from entering very deeply into the mental universe of the Cartesians. And though he wholeheartedly embraced atomistic mechanism, he did not venture beyond its general principle that, in the realm of matter – that is to say, extension – everything is a result of the configuration and motion of the elementary particles.

Bayle was much more strongly attracted by the Cartesian method, and especially by the way it could be used to distinguish between propositions which, since they remained unaffected by systematic doubt, had the status of self-evident truths, and others which were merely examples of gratuitous word-spinning. The Cartesian method is one that leaves only a few tiny nuggets in the prospector's sieve, and throws away copious quantities of sand. Since it leaves one aware of the vast number of problems that can never be solved, or have still to be properly posed, it is a sceptical method. Complete scepticism, however, leaves everything in doubt, whereas Descartes used it simply as a means of suspending judgement until he had discovered the few fundamental truths which doubt could not undermine, and on which he could build a positive system of ideas. Descartes himself, and Malebranche after him, discarded whole areas of human knowledge, including historical knowledge. Bayle, with his passion for history, refused to go to such lengths. Instead, he tried to adapt the method so that it could be used to separate the true from the false in the field of historical erudition. The historian's task, as he saw it, was to weigh the claims of the various written records, pick out what they have in common, resolve their contradictions by using conjecture, and thus establish, bit by bit, a degree of probability for the alleged fact which in some cases – such as the existence of the historical Julius Caesar – may be accorded the status of a certainty. Such historical certainty Bayle sees as the equivalent of Cartesian self-evidence, but unlike Descartes who had no place for the merely probable in his theory of knowledge, Bayle (who was no mathematician) regards historical certainty as the last step on a scale of increasing probabilities.

The greatest lesson Bayle learned from Cartesianism was to rid himself of a naïve trust in first impressions. In the field of history, as so often elsewhere, he was a populariser. The humanists and the Benedictines had already elaborated quite sophisticated methods of textual criticism, but Bayle made a whole programme of source-criticism accessible to a wide public. The source-critic has to track down in his documents what are later accretions, to spot the errors, of omission as well as commission, of the copyists, and to take into account the mistakes that have been made in translating, dating and attributing the manuscripts. It is a cardinal principle that historical erudition should be evaluated in terms of the weight of the evidence, not its quantity. A credible witness of an event is one who was present when it occurred, for if a story has been retold several times, it becomes hopelessly inaccurate, at least in its details. A true critical approach does not take the crude line that a testimony is either truthful or a lie. It seeks out the witness behind the testimony, and takes account of the possibility that even though perfectly sincere he may be inaccurate without realising it, filling in gaps in his memory by referring to his imagination or, still worse, his preconceptions, and acting throughout in the good faith which thus, though a necessary condition of veracity, is far from being a sufficient one. Even an eyewitness, in principle the most authoritative sort, is bound to be biased, without realising it, by the very fact of his involvement in the event he is describing (it may, for example, be a battle in which he has fought).

Bayle often takes his examples from Maimbourg and his followers, who used tendentious accounts of the Wars of Religion to justify the anti-Huguenot policies of the French Court a century later. These supposed works of history, which many readers believed to be factually accurate, were really thinly disguised works of controversy. Similarly, those who had imagined that the recent proliferation of gazettes would provide plenty of reliable source material for the future historian, were due to have their hopes dashed. Authors of gazettes are often rogues, and their readers dupes; in any case they are all prone to believe anything that appeals to them. If we compare works on the same topic by historians of different creeds or nationalities, or gazettes from different countries (as Bayle had managed to do in Geneva, and could now do in Holland) it is clear that they reflect the allegiance of the writer or are shamelessly the voices of government propaganda. 'History is dished up very much like meat ... Each nation and each religion takes the same raw facts and dresses them in a sauce of its own taste, and each reader finds them true or false according to whether they agree or disagree with his prejudices' (*NRL* Mar. 1686, iv). The 'base hacks' who write the gazettes, Bayle describes as not just 'harpies who sully everything they touch' but also as 'executioners

who twist the neck, the arms and the legs of historical facts, and
sometimes even cut them off and replace them by artificial ones'
('Discourse on the pamphlets', vii, in *Dict.*)

Bayle's paradoxes

In the wholesale inaccuracy and untrustworthiness of the documents he cites, Bayle finds evidence not so much of man's
intellectual incapacity as of his moral weakness. 'The obstacles
to objective judgement do not come from a mind that is
ignorant but from one that is full of prejudices' (*Dict.* Pellisson,
in text). Historical criticism leaves us with an image of man
which is strikingly similar to that of Calvinist theology: we are
all incurable sinners; not only our actions but our judgements
are determined by our passions, and the fact that we are often
unaware of this makes the consequences even worse.

It is in this perspective that we should see what for many
readers seemed to be Bayle's most notorious 'paradox' – the
assertion that atheists are not a social menace, and that a society
composed only of atheists would be perfectly viable. 'It is no
more strange that an Atheist should lead a virtuous life, than
that a Christian should commit any kind of crime' – this last
being a fact of experience. Convinced as he was that human
beings are incapable of putting their theoretical beliefs into
practice if this means making even the slightest effort to
dominate their inclinations, Bayle cannot see that the atheist is
in any worse case than the type of Christian who confesses God
'with his lips and not with his heart', that is, than the overwhelming majority of Christians (as a Calvinist, Bayle believed
that only a tiny élite possess the living faith that truly sanctifies).
All, whether atheists or 'lip-serving Christians', are motivated in
their conduct by their 'temperament', in other words by their
passions as conditioned by their upbringing. Even so, it is a fact
of observation that the depravity of human beings in no way
makes communal life impossible. This is because, though
knowledge of the basic principle of morality, the law of reciprocity which forbids me to do to others what I would not have them
do to me, may not be the inner motive of my conduct, it is
nevertheless the yardstick by which I judge others and know

that I am judged by them. Provided therefore that it does not positively go counter to my dominant passion (and it will not always do so, for no man has all the vices all the time), I will do out of concern for my reputation and fear of punishment – in other words out of the vice of self-love – that which I am incapable of doing through an inner sense of moral obligation.

It is clear from this that Bayle sees actions performed out of enlightened self-interest or at the dictate of the 'point of honour' as devoid of moral significance. Honesty, therefore, cannot be 'the best policy' precisely because honesty has nothing to do with a policy. None of this, however, makes any difference to the conditions of social life, which only require us to behave more or less in accordance with moral principles, and makes no enquiry as to motives. Now, it is self-evident that an atheist need not be less responsive to the exigences of the 'point of honour' or to enlightened self-interest than a believer. Hence he is capable of being just as good a citizen. Bayle does not deny that any society must guard against its own disintegration, and that a 'repressive principle' is therefore necessary. Yet for the great majority of men it is not the fear of God that performs this function, but fear of imminent and palpable punishments here on earth (Hell, on the other hand, seems a long way off ...), and the desire for praise and esteem.

Bayle accompanies this first 'paradox' with another, which seemed equally disconcerting to his contemporaries, who were comfortably at home with the notion that suffering in the after-life (and hence religion itself) was a vital factor in ensuring social order. They insisted that Christianity alone could attain this end, oblivious of the fact that numerous stable and prosperous societies had never heard of Christianity. Bayle argues that if there were a society (such as has never in fact been) composed entirely of regenerate Christians who all genuinely practised the Gospel ethic, it would never last: its less scrupulous neighbours would soon wipe out a community which refused on principle to soil its hands with the base practices of diplomacy or to cultivate those 'warlike' virtues that are so clearly incompatible with love of one's neighbour. Bayle's parable is a cruel illustration of human corruption. On the other hand, if his imaginary

Christian community were isolated from others, as in the utopian romances popular in his day, no internal flaw would exist to stop it from flourishing. Once again, this is a Protestant way of seeing things, one in which celibacy is not the ideal. Bayle's symmetrical paradoxes have their roots in Protestant moral rigorism. Not only do what is moral and what is useful not coincide, but they are often mutually antagonistic. Nevertheless, the useful is enough by itself to ensure an ordered society. This is a point which was later to be developed by the English satirist Mandeville, in *The Fable of the Bees* (1714).

It is important to underline the particular sense in which Bayle holds that speculative notions do not influence human conduct; this is only true when such notions contradict a man's natural inclinations. But when theory agrees with inclinations, it reinforces their effects. This is why fanaticism is such a scourge. The conviction that you are fighting the Lord's battle and winning the approval of your peers opens the way for injustice and cruelty on the vastest scale, as is shown by the atrocities perpetrated in 'holy wars' like the Crusades and the Wars of Religion. Ideas may have no influence in controlling our passions, but they are all too capable of aggravating our vices and giving them the colour of virtue, and with it social respectability.

The theological approach

Bayle has a particular conception of the attributes of the divinity, without which the First Cause cannot be called God. Thanks to his upbringing, Bayle's image of God is more religious than metaphysical. His divinity is a tutelary God. A God on the Epicurean or deistic model, who did not enter into a special relationship with some of his human creatures, did not answer their prayers, and did not act providentially, could not be a god at all. Bayle found in the Bible the notion of a good and all-powerful God who entered into an alliance with men, the God of Abraham, Isaac and Jacob, someone who was not the Supreme Being or the Great Geometer, but He to whom man can turn in his distress, whose Spirit bloweth where it listeth, and who assures of eternal salvation those whom He has mysteriously chosen out of the great mass of the lost souls who make up sinful humanity. God is a hidden God, the transcendent object of faith rather than the object of philosophical reason.

In these circumstances, the problem of the existence of God is best understood as ground on which believers and atheists are locked in struggle, with concern for one's opponent and efforts of persuasion taking precedence over rigorous dialectic and demonstrative proofs. Metaphysical proofs of God's existence lead only to an abstract idea of God, not to a person one can fear and love. This explains Bayle's cavalier attitude towards the Cartesian proofs of the existence of what Pascal called 'the God of the philosophers and scholars', and the fact that, diverging widely from the Cartesian standpoint, he continues to use the time-honoured a posteriori argument which proves God's existence from the order and beauty of the Creation. The Heavens proclaim the glory of God, and the universal clock attests the existence of the Clockmaker. Bayle is aware that this is not a rigorous logical proof, but he sees it as a persuasive one. Above all it has the advantage in his eyes of refuting the kind of materialist argument which ascribes the order of the cosmos to pure chance. In other words, it is not so much a positive proof as one that negates a particular form of atheism. This, however, is characteristic of philosophical proofs. Since God is the object of faith, only a revelation can positively assure us of His existence. In this Bayle directly echoes Calvin.

As God is thought of as having a personal relationship with man, with whom he makes a covenant, based on promises and duties, it is easy to understand why Bayle thinks it less offensive to deny specific attributes to God (even including that of existence), than to credit Him falsely with attributes that are unworthy and that dishonour Him. Hence, following Plutarch and Bacon, Bayle maintains that the atheist who does not know God offends Him less than the idolator who acknowledges more than one god, attributes immoral conduct to his own deity, worships him in a manner that is often cruel or indecent (and always ludicrous), and even, in some instances, demeans him to a level below that of an animal, that of inert matter. Since a man of honour would rather be thought wrongly to be dead than be credited with infamous conduct, it follows that atheism is less scandalous than idolatry. This is the underlying theme of the *Miscellaneous Reflections on the Comet*, as well as of other works. It is not surprising that Bayle, a fundamentally reasonable man of his times as well as a Protestant brought up on the Old Testament, should so scorn – almost, one could say, abominate – polytheism. In any case, it is obvious that the work is not the anachronistic attack on classical paganism which it at first seems to be, but a thinly disguised piece of anti-Catholic polemics: 'idolatry' was the term Protestants used for worship of the Virgin, the saints, holy relics and the adoration of the Host.

Fideism and scepticism

Bayle thus discusses intellectual issues on two different levels, the rational and the theological. At one time, around 1685–6, under Malebranche's influence, he thought that the two could be reconciled, but this soon proved to have been an illusion, and from then on he regarded them as incompatible and contradictory. Bayle was familiar with the major metaphysical systems of his day, and took over some of their doctrines. In particular, he accepted Descartes's dualism, which radically separated thought and matter. But there is little point in trying to use any of these doctrines to evaluate his intellectual position. It is more to the point, given his own preference for theological themes, to think of him as a theologian. A theologian looks to revelation and not to human reason for the ultimate answer to questions about the world and man. A Protestant theologian, in particular, sees reason as simply an auxiliary of revelation, its task being limited to setting forth the transcendental truths, which it is powerless to discover for itself, since they come from another source altogether.

Religious fideism rather than metaphysical scepticism is the primary factor in Bayle's emphasis on the limitations and contradictions of human reason. Fideism means having recourse to divine revelation, which furnishes man with truths which are incomprehensible to his reason and not susceptible of rational demonstration, but are accepted through trust in the veracity of their source. 'In religious matters, the rule of judgement does not lie in the intellect but in the conscience, which means that we should accept things . . . on the grounds that our conscience tells us that in so doing we shall be doing what is agreeable to God' (*NLGC* xxii xiii). Furthermore, if one believes, as Bayle does, that 'everything which seems to us not to be in conformity with reason, must seem to be contrary to reason' (*RPQ* ii clix), then reason and the Christian mysteries actually contradict one another. We may think that religion simply extends the perceptions of everyday experience, but this is not so. The truths of religion transcend reason, and the only way to enter their domain is to abandon everyday common sense, engage in a wager, and make a perilous leap of faith.

Bayle's particular religious upbringing led him to postulate that God has spoken to us in the Bible, which reveals 'what we should believe . . . and what we should do' (*Dict*. Pyrrhon n. C). Under the influence of the great Catholic exegetist Richard Simon (1636–1712) Bayle weaned himself away from the literal interpretation of the Bible on which he had been reared. The text of Holy Scripture can be analysed by the critical methods which humanist scholarship has devised for the study of the literature of pagan antiquity. Human contingency has left its mark on the Biblical text, not just in the material circumstances of its transmission by copyists capable of making mistakes, but also in its content: 'the popular mind not being able to rise to the sublime height of the Supremely Perfect Being, the prophets had to bring God down to human level and make him speak to us in the way a nursemaid speaks to a child she suckles' (*Dict*. Rimini (Grégoire de) n. B). It is pointless to look for astronomical or physical truths in the Bible, or even for philosophical propositions. It was not Christ's purpose to 'back up one group of philosophers in their arguments with the rest' but to 'confound all philosophy and demonstrate its vanity . . . just as his Gospel seemed like foolishness to the philosophers, so he wanted philosophy to seem like foolishness to Christians' (*Dict*. Third Clarification, ii).

Bayle's tone in writing about various Old Testament figures in his *Dictionary* is the reverse of humble and pious. Of the story of the Fall, he writes:

No undertaking was ever as important, since the destiny of the whole of humanity for all time was at stake ... and yet no matter was ever completed so swiftly ... it must be admitted that the two creatures to whom God had confided the salvation of mankind could not have looked after it worse ... they put up less resistance than a child when someone is trying to take away its doll. (*Dict*. Eve n. A)

Bayle's irreverent manner has led many readers to conclude that he must, as time went on, have lost his belief in the religious significance of the Bible. This is perhaps too extreme a view. In fact, the most obviously flippant of his comments are confined to a few passages of the Pentateuch over which floods of ink had already been spilled well before his time. Nor did he simply invent the often ludicrous questions to which he gave offhand and provocative answers, such as Sara's exact age when her beauty prompted Abimelech to abduct her. Questions such as these had been the subject of learned commentaries *ad nauseam*, and Bayle may well have been directing his irony not against the Bible itself, but against its innumerable rabbinical and Christian commentators. Where Voltaire would certainly have mocked, Bayle may only have been joking, rather in the manner of a burlesque work like Scarron's *Aeneid Travestied*, which was written to entertain rather than with the aim of denigrating Virgil. As for the contentious article on 'David', we should note that when he underlines the faults of the prophet-king, Bayle is only being faithful to the sacred text, which neither conceals nor excuses them. Bayle writes that

the profound respect which we owe to this great king and prophet should not prevent us from expressing our disapproval of the occasions on which he went astray; otherwise, we should be giving the profane the chance to assert that any action is justified if it is performed by a person we revere. Nothing could be more harmful to Christian morality. It is vital for true religion that the way of life of those who profess it should be judged by universal criteria of uprightness and order. (*Dict*. David n. D)

Bayle's point in writing this article, as Walter Rex has convincingly shown (see 'Further reading'), was to express in a guarded way his reservations about a contemporary ruler, William III, whose panegyrists often compared him with David.

On the one hand, Bayle abandoned the simplistic conception of the literal inspiration of the Bible; on the other hand, Simon's influence, reinforcing traditional Protestant exegesis, steered him away from allegorical interpretation, which Simon disparagingly called 'mystiquerie'. Similarly, with the down-to-earth outlook of the typical 'reasonable man' of his day, he was impervious to the appeal of classical mythology. All he could see in it were its inaccuracies (in the instances where it overlapped with history) and its contradictions, while he came nowhere near to perceiving that it might be an outgrowth of popular, local, traditions. He was thus unlikely to have any kind of sympathy for the time-honoured stories of the Pentateuch, and the fact is not one that he tried to conceal. Even so, the view that the Bible was supernaturally inspired had a tremendous weight of tradition behind it, and it would be rash to assert that Bayle had entirely thrown it off.

The one path Bayle never took, as he steered a course between the temptation of faith on the one hand and unbelief on the other, was that of deism. Deists believed only in God as the Great Architect of the Universe, and (some of them) in the immortality of the soul. Bayle could see nothing that was in any meaningful sense religious about the idea of God as Universal Architect, and he was clear in his view that human reason, left to itself, could never establish that the soul either was, or was not, immortal. The deistic concept of a 'reasonable religion' was therefore meaningless for him. Faith and reason, as he saw it, never come into contact. Nevertheless, Bayle did see in reason a way of supporting faith by, as it were, creating a vacuum for it. His stance reminds us that scepticism and fideism have a good deal in common, both historically and doctrinally, and that it cannot be argued that because scepticism undermines purely rational conviction it necessarily leads only to unbelief. It is impossible to draw a firm line between blind faith, experienced existentially, and scepticism used irreverently: the two coexist in a constantly changing relationship which makes interpretation difficult, just as much — it is worth noting — in the case of Bayle as in that of Montaigne, about whose religious outlook specialists are still hopelessly divided.

Despite this, most commentators have refused to take seriously the notion that, in calling himself a Christian, Bayle may have been perfectly sincere. Their simplistic view of religious psychology makes no allowance for the fact that states of mind fluctuate, or for the ambiguous workings of subconscious motivation. But when Bayle writes as follows, he must surely be speaking from personal experience:

> there are ... people whose religion is in the heart, and not in the mind. The moment they seek it by human reasoning, they lose sight of it; it eludes the subtleties and sophistries of their processes of argument; when they try to weight up the pros and cons, they become confused; but as soon as they stop arguing, and simply listen to the evidence of their feelings, the instinctive promptings of their conscience, the legacy of their upbringing, and so on, they are convinced by a religion and live their lives by it, so far as human infirmity allows. (*Dict.* Spinoza n. M)

4 What Bayle argued against

The problem of evil

Bayle was a vociferous champion of fideism, which enabled him to riddle theological systems with insidious objections. These were aimed not at revealed dogmas such as the Trinity, the Incarnation or the Resurrection, but at the pitiable efforts of theologians to try to prove that these beliefs were not, as Bayle held, fundamentally inexplicable, and that they could be squared with the demands of reason. 'Were reason in agreement with itself,' Bayle wrote,

> then it would indeed be regrettable that we find it so difficult to reconcile it with some of our articles of faith. But that is not the case. Reason is like a runner who doesn't know that the race is over, or, like Penelope, constantly undoing what it creates ... It is better suited to pulling things down than to building them up, and better at discovering what things are not, than what they are. (*RQP* ii cxxxvii)

Most later readers have believed that when Bayle called the coherence of Christian theology in question, he was trying to undermine Christianity itself. It is much more likely that he was not engaging in anti-Christian polemics at all, but in inter-confessional controversy. His writings can be seen as a kind of postscript to the furious debates in the sixteenth century when the different Churches were ranged against one another. What loosened the hold of Christianity on the Western world was not so much attacks from outside (for example, as a result of developments in modern science) as violent dissension within. The combatants became so adept at hurling insults at their brethren that, even though they had only set out to refute the arguments of fellow-Christians with whom they happened to disagree, they unwittingly succeeded in weakening Christianity itself.

When Bayle began to discuss the problem of evil, he may

have been motivated by the desire to defend Calvinism against the bitter reproaches of other schools of Christian theology, all of which accused the Protestants of espousing the sacrilegious thesis that 'God is the author of sin.' Like Calvin, Bayle denied that any theodicy – that is to say, any theory that would explain rationally how God's omnipotence and goodness could be reconciled with the fact of evil in the world – was possible. There can, he argues, be no way of demonstrating that the all-powerful Creator should not be held responsible for the evils that disfigure his creation. Christians have to accept, precisely because they are Christians, that God is holy and good, just as they have to accept, as a fact of experience, that evil is everywhere. How both these things can be so is something that the human mind is not capable either of imagining or of understanding. It must suffice that the Bible tells us that God is both holy and all-powerful. It is evident that, far from trying to water down Calvin's 'hard saying', Bayle in one sense upholds the view of which he was accused. God is indeed 'the author of sin' for, having foreseen everything as well as created everything, he is responsible for everything that happens in creation – not just for what he causes to happen, but for what he allows to happen as well. Christians have to accept, as something which passes comprehension, that the omnipresence of evil does not detract in any way from God's sanctity.

Bayle in fact engages in elaborate arguments to prove, with great virtuosity, that no other Christian theology here fares any better than Calvin's. The problem of evil is a mystery, the idea of a mystery is an integral part of the Christian faith, and if this were to be deemed not to be so, Christianity itself would crumble into ruins. If the Calvinists are unpopular with other Christians, it is because they say out loud, frankly and unambiguously, what others know they must believe, but try to conceal beneath a flood of verbiage.

However it was not only, or even primarily, because it seemed a particularly propitious ground for controversy that Bayle was attracted to the problem of evil. It had tormented him ceaselessly since the death of his brother Jacob had shattered the naïve confidence he had felt in his younger days in the workings of divine Providence. He traced the nub of the problem to the inevitable contradiction between a theocentric view of human existence, and the actual experience of evil and suffering. For evil to be intelligible, in other words for a theodicy to be possible, one had to adopt the point of view of God and to see everything on a universal scale. The most Bayle believed it possible to say was that as a matter of faith God does indeed take a positive view of the reality of human experience, but that this view is inaccessible to us. This being the case, we should declare a moratorium on the use of human reasoning. When, as we must, we call God holy, just and good, we should realise that these terms cannot have their purely human sense.

However, Bayle was also a great admirer of Grotius (1587–1648), the founder of the Protestant Natural Law School, who held that moral imperatives had the status of rational intuitions. Reason thus tells us that to give to each his own, to do unto others as one would be done unto oneself, to keep one's word, and so forth, are not only logical propositions but moral imperatives. Bayle believed that the basic moral commands are engraved on the human mind so deeply that even a 'speculative atheist' (a very different being from the 'practising atheist' steeped in vice) cannot ignore them, for they are even more strongly entrenched than the idea of God itself. Hence Bayle has no doubts about judging the kind of statements theologians make about God's behaviour by the standards of human morality. Indeed, he was unlikely to be taxed with anthropomorphism since it was commonplace for theologians themselves to demonstrate God's wisdom and goodness by comparing him to a king, a master, or a father. However, Bayle's own way of using such comparisons has the effect of showing how impossible it is to understand the mystery of divine transcendence. We might be tempted to argue that God was obliged to permit evil in order to respect the free will with which he had endowed Adam and his descendants. But, Bayle writes,

No good mother who has given her daughters permission to go to a ball would not withdraw her consent if she were to know for certain that they would lose their virginity there, and any mother who did know that for certain, and let them go after exhorting them to be good, and threatening them with punishment if they failed to return home virgins, would be justly convicted of loving neither her daughters nor chastity ... How unwise it is, then, to argue that God was obliged to respect Adam's free will. (*Dict.* Pauliciens n. E)

All the major confessions agreed that, the divinity being both omniscient and prescient, evil was the inevitable price man had to pay for the supreme good of free will. Bayle, once again, finds this an easy argument to refute. All Christians agree that divine grace does not supersede human freedom, but co-operates with it (the only differences of opinion are about how it does this). Hence, God could have given Adam the grace not to sin, and still respected his free will. Adam would still have been a finite creature, with a potential freedom to choose sin, but this freedom could have remained unrealised.

Bayle also examined the implications of the dilemma formulated by Epicurus, who had claimed that either God had not wanted to prevent evil, which cast doubt on his goodness, or he was incapable of doing so, which put his omnipotence in question. It was in this perspective that the Socinians had taken up the problem. They argued that God simply made the universe out of pre-existent matter, but that he did so without possessing foreknowledge, so that the disobedience of Adam and Eve came, so to speak, as a surprise to him. This preserves the concept of God's goodness, but only at the cost of drastically limiting his power and wisdom. Bayle argues that, if God had the slightest thought that the Fall might occur, he should, given the appalling consequences we know followed, have let the original chaos subsist rather than create the world we have.

With this argument, Bayle shifts the discussion of the problem of evil on to a new plane. Since the Creation *ex nihilo* is a dogmatic assertion, it is wrong to postulate a 'nature of things' capable of resisting the Creator's will. If sin and evil exist, God has willed them; they are not forces that frustrate his plans. What this more metaphysical approach does is to underline the disparity between the notions of divine goodness and divine wisdom. Goodness envisages man's eternal salvation, while wisdom sees that the universe functions according to fixed general laws (or, in another version, that it represents the best choice of possibilities God could have made – in Leibniz's view, the least bad). The sufferings of the just on earth and the damned in the world to come may thus seem to indicate that God has sacrificed his goodness to his wisdom. But this is only because, without realising it, we are thinking of God as being faced with a 'nature of things' analogous to that postulated by the Platonic or Socinian concept of the divinity: a God who has to reckon and compromise with the resistance of pre-existent matter. Whether this nature of things is thought of as forming a part of God, as present to his mind as a possibility, or as existing outside him, makes no difference. We have still reduced the Omnipotent One to the status of a craftsman working with rebellious matter. And this in turn means that God's transcendence has been subordinated to the concept of a blind Necessity.

Bayle began to discuss the problem of evil in the *Dictionary*, and continued it in the *Reply to the Questions of a Provincial*, where he engaged in argument with Jean Le Clerc. Le Clerc had tried to attenuate the force of Bayle's observations by abandoning the dogma that the torments of the damned are eternal. If all men are eventually assured of eternal beatitude, then Hell is only temporary and its harshness need no longer appal us. Bayle lost no time in exploiting this unwise concession on his opponent's part. If it is incompatible with God's sovereign goodness to believe that sinners will suffer eternal punishment after death, it is easy to show that the same can be argued of punishment of any duration. Step by step, Bayle's inexorable logic leads him to conclude that, on his opponent's premiss, even if Hell did not exist, the fact of earthly sufferings alone would be sufficient to negate the supreme goodness which it is our religious duty to ascribe to God. If none the less we do affirm His goodness, it can only be through an act of faith, never as the result of a 'rational' deduction.

All this makes clear how foreign the deep-rooted metaphysical optimism of the whole Western tradition was to Bayle's way of thinking. For Bayle, the life of an individual human being holds more evil than good, and it would have been better not to have been born – as Jesus said of Judas – for everyone. Bayle is so obsessed by a sense of the wastefulness of the Creation, as witnessed by the wretchedness of life on earth and the eternal torments in store for the damned, that he finds it impossible to give any credence to the orthodox view that a good God, though in a position to know how much His goodness would have to be subordinated to His wisdom, nevertheless went ahead and created our world. From the outset, Bayle refuses to see things in these terms. He has no intention of saying to the Divine Potter, 'Why have you made me as I am?', being only too well aware that there are any number of clever metaphysical answers to the question. What he does though is to rebuke the Divinity with a question which expects no answer: 'Why have you created me at all?'

Bayle's savage criticisms of all attempts to construct a theodicy, criticisms which had lost none of their pertinence when Leibniz tried to counter them after Bayle's death, are exceptional in the history of European ideas. The miserable worm that is man may be submissive, but he is not resigned. Instead of automatically identifying himself with God's point of view, he dares to speak up for his own. When Bayle insists that he never asked to be cast into this vale of tears in the first place, he completely undermines the whole basis of the argument about evil: in fact, he makes it pointless even to broach the question, since evil is no longer, as in the traditional view, the context in which God acts, but the very stuff of the Creation. Bayle can be compared here with the Buddhists, denying the characteristically Western assumption that Being is the supreme good, disclaiming man's will to live, and suggesting that perhaps non-being would be preferable.

We should not be surprised, therefore, if Bayle's fideism sometimes seems strained. When his instincts tell him that existence may be valueless, the only way he can believe in God's wisdom and goodness is through an act of faith. However, an such an act did not come easily to Bayle. There was too great a gap between divine omnipotence and divine goodness, and it was only revelation which prevented life from being like a metaphysical nightmare: one in which an all-powerful Spirit of Evil manipulates its creatures like puppets on a string, a cosmic Nero treating the whole universe as a spectacle for his amusement. Grotesque though this passing image may be, it reflects not only Bayle's own temperament but what Huguenot communities saw as the disaster visited on them by history, and the underlying sense of failure felt by so many of the refugees.

Dualism as an answer

It is not surprising, given the religious character of Bayle's sensibility and upbringing, that in his efforts to render God innocent of responsibility for human suffering he should find himself exploring heretical ideas. His commitment to the idea of divine goodness was too strong for him to be content with the colourless notion of a Cosmic Architect who creates the universe by overcoming the passive resistance of pre-existent matter. This would leave God with the terrible responsibility of creating something even worse than the original Chaos, in which unformed matter at least could not be said to have caused conscious beings to suffer. To uphold the innocence of the Principle of Good, dualism has to be pressed to the point of postulating the existence of a Principle of Evil. Then God's intervention would only have taken place to limit the damage which another Being was responsible for, and to win back some of that Being's gains. In the articles of the *Dictionary* in which he rehabilitates the traditionally despised and misunderstood heretical dualists of old, the Manicheans and the Paulicians, Bayle reconstructs their doctrines with considerable sympathy. It was, in any case, typical of him to take the side of some of the less popular figures of history and, stimulated by the paucity and the hostility of the available sources, to restore their arguments by conjecture. Many of Bayle's readers assumed that he was defending heresy, and were scandalised. Once again, this was an over-hasty reaction. Although Bayle presents a posteriori arguments for dualism which make it seem convincing, and compatible with divine sanctity, he still believes that the oneness of the Divinity can be demonstrated on metaphysical grounds. He no doubt regarded his sympathetic treatment of the dualists as a useful weapon against the 'rationalists', and felt that by reviving the devastating objections of the Manicheans, he could confound their facile optimism. His own professed attitude is one of neutrality.

As a fideist, he stands on the sidelines, above the battle, proclaiming the need to affirm unambiguously, and in a spirit of piety, that God is both good and all-powerful, while at the same time abjuring any attempt to imagine how these two attributes, which in the light of reason are contradictory, can be reconciled. This said, and for the particular benefit of those who (wrongly) refuse to submit their reason to the yoke of faith, Bayle gives the palm to the dualists, and takes a malicious pleasure in mortifying his real, living opponents by the amount of space he gives to the despised heretics of former times. Not surprisingly, Le Clerc took umbrage and Jurieu was outraged at the spectacle of Bayle clothing himself in fideistic affirmations of unimpeachable Calvinistic orthodoxy. As a result, Bayle's various enemies were encouraged to sink their differences and to join ranks in branding him as a nauseating hypocrite whose professions of piety were merely a cloak to hide the scandal of his atheism.

Bayle's metaphysical positions

To use such language about Bayle is to substitute insults for objective judgements, the more so since it tells us nothing about the particular character of his supposed 'atheism'. Even if we discount Bayle's own professions of fideism, there is still evidence of his inner beliefs that requires interpretation. As well as being more favourable to Manicheanism than to deistic optimism, we find that Bayle is also implacably opposed to metaphysical materialism, and hence to what was really meant by atheism in his day. Like Descartes, with whom he was here entirely in agreement, Bayle conceived of matter as inert extension. Hence he rejected the materialist view which, in line with seventeenth-century thinking, he identified with a form of atomism. All order, Bayle argues, emanates from an organising mind, simultaneously aware of the ends it is pursuing and the means of achieving them – Bayle dismissed as absurd the Epicurean theory that the ordered universe we know came into being as the result of the chance collision of atoms. How, though, can the organising mind, which is pure spirit by definition, act on extended matter? How can one join together what has been so sharply put asunder? Here Bayle follows Malebranche in arguing that this is something that only the Creator, in His relationship with His creation, can do. The Creator alone can move the matter He has created, and all second causes are only 'occasional', in other words pseudo-causes. This point of view was to be remembered by Hume, though without taking over Malebranche's solution of making God alone a cause in the full sense of the term.

Occasionalism may seem a strange doctrine for Bayle to espouse, but it fitted well with his resolute hostility towards any attempt to suggest that God was immanent in Creation, and not transcendent over it. We have an example of this in his debate with Jean Le Clerc on the theory of the 'plastic natures' which the Cambridge Platonists had proposed as intermediary principles between God and the material universe. Bayle does not doubt the piety of those who propounded this thesis, but he does question the soundness of their metaphysics. Any philosophy of immanence, he argues, is ultimately reducible to materialism. If you ascribe to a principle immanent in matter any part of the organisation of the material world, however small, you have provided a loophole through which the idea of a transcendent Creator will quickly disappear altogether. It is characteristic of Bayle to have no use for half-measures. Only extreme positions strike him as coherent. Either you hold, as a materialist, that movement and order are inherent in matter, or you invoke a spiritual cause, in which case this can only be a god who is transcendent, creates, and is in the strictest sense supernatural. In this way Bayle, with what is almost a caricature of the consequences of Cartesian dualism as he understood it, rejects immanentism or vitalism of any kind, any recourse to occult forces, any theory of the gradual actualisation of potentialities, and any notion of inner dynamism.

Bayle also believes that he has an immediate and insuperable answer to deism. If deism simply means assuming that a divine organising principle has fashioned matter which is co-eternal with it and which, so to speak, it had before its eyes, what means could this hypothetical divinity have of acting on something that is totally alien to it? The breach between God and matter, created by the dualistic distinction of thought and extension, is so radical that it can only be bridged by invoking the mystery of the relationship of the Creator with His creatures. The Great Architect of the Universe is necessarily also its creator, but revelation is needed to characterise him as all-powerful or all-good. The God of the deists is not God the Father or God the Saviour, and has nothing to offer that might inspire love or praise: on the contrary, He deserves only our curses for having made man a mere cog in His vast machine. In the way Bayle denounces the God of the deists as not simply a pale copy, but an odious counterfeit, of the Christian God, he reveals the continuing influence of his pious childhood, and of the warm and secure trust in God's paternal providence in which he grew up.

Bayle does not so much contest the deists' actual arguments as the strictly religious implications to which they point. In his own thinking, he seems to oscillate between the extreme poles of an intransigent view of Christianity, and the nightmare vision of a Universe created by a Supreme Being who may not be – since these things cannot be proved – good, moral or capable of pity for His creatures. Yet if Bayle really did see things in such starkly alternative terms, one may wonder why he did not speak with the accents of a Luther or a Kierkegaard. It is not easy to believe that beneath his jaunty tone and offhand manner there lurks a sense of anguish. The answer perhaps is that the choice Bayle offers us between a God who is paternal, and one who is indifferent to His creatures, and therefore a cruel God, only affects our speculative ideas, without any practical consequences flowing from it. The categorical imperative of morality remains the same whether it has God's backing or not. At the same time, it is not subordinated to utility: what is 'moral' is often the exact opposite of what is 'useful'. Morality is incompatible with egoism or subjectivism, since it is founded on reason and reciprocity, and involves abnegation. By making morality autonomous in this way (and thus incidentally foreshadowing Kant, another Protestant by upbringing), Bayle frees us to live our lives without commitment to any metaphysical system. Speculation becomes simply a harmless game, and however much a sceptic may vacillate in his opinions, this need not disturb his serenity. While dogmatic systems are tossed around like fragile barks by the tempests of doubt, the realm of moral values is a rock of certitude which stands firm against the storms which beat around it.

Between Bayle's pessimism about life in the here and now, and the autonomy he ascribes to morality, there is a correlation. He sees any connection between virtue and happiness as being purely extrinsic. If God wipes away all our tears in the afterlife, this implies that He reverses, not that He prolongs and ameliorates, the course of our earthly life. But this is not something that we can claim is presupposed by, or deducible from, our earthly experience, and optimism can therefore only be founded on revelation. Bayle cannot forgive his rationalist opponents for presenting optimism as an obvious and readily accessible point of view, for this wholly fails to grasp the tragic depth of the enigma of Evil, any more than he can forgive those Christian theologians who are naïve and unintelligent enough glibly to connect the hand of Providence with particular events here on earth.

Bayle's hesitations

The apparent complacency with which Bayle refrains from taking up a definite position on any problems of the kind which no philosophical system can afford to leave open, is the corollary of his genuine metaphysical scepticism. Out of scholarly modesty rather than mental laziness he performs dazzling arabesques around most of the burning issues of his day, without ever coming to a conclusion. On free will, for instance, he is prepared to accept the testimony of common sense, while at the same time admitting the plausibility of determinism. Another example of his suspension of judgement, or acceptance of the fact that speculative reasoning has no way of coming to terms with reality, is the question of the souls of animals, a much-debated topic on which Bayle had gathered a vast amount of data. To regard animals as machines, as Descartes did, is to avoid some awkward problems. What kind of soul is it that is not immortal? If all living things are capable of suffering, and if animals possess consciousness as well as men, does this not aggravate the problem of Evil and add to the iniquity of the sufferings of the innocent? Where do we draw the line? – do worms have souls? At the same time, our natural instincts rebel against the idea that a dog may be just like a watch, an ingenious assembly of cog-wheels put together by a divine craftsman.

The same refusal to reach a conclusion marks Bayle's discussion of the nature of the physical continuum, which some say consists of elementary particles or atoms, while others regard it as an infinitely divisible whole; similarly with his discussion of the existence of a vacuum, declared by Descartes to be impossible a priori, but claimed by others to have been demonstrated experimentally. Everything about Bayle – his fertile imagination where abstractions are concerned, his extensive reading, and his chosen mode of expression – is conducive to his habit of flitting from one problem to another, and coming up in the process with a multitude of penetrating insights and unexpected connections. Sometimes, too, his thinking has an oddly archaic flavour. Thus he considers it plausible to suppose that the trajectory of the celestial bodies is governed by angels, and that other members of the heavenly host direct the transformation of the embryo from an imperceptible egg into a completely formed animal. Bayle was quite aware of the new horizons opened up to physiology by the invention of the microscope. If he takes up the thesis of the activity of angels, probably expanding here Malebranche's more cautions views, it is because he needs it to fill a gap left by his loss of faith in the extreme Cartesian claim to explain *every* material phenomenon in terms of the laws of movement and collision.

By not setting up as a systematic thinker, he could afford not to synthesise his ideas, and on more than one occasion he lets a discussion drop just as his reader has begun to wonder what is coming next. His lack of earnestness is doubtless one of the reasons why he appeals to the modern reader. There is an underlying unity to his writings, but it has more to do with style than with content, with his horror of the kind of blinkered dogmatism which consistently underrates possible objections, and with the daring way in which he puts forward bold hypotheses.Bayle performed the same kind of service for philosophy as he did for history, by continually demonstrating its limitations, attacking its blind reliance on commonplaces, and encouraging daring speculation. In this way, he prepared the ground for Hume and Kant.

Bayle was also a precursor of what was to become the history of philosophy. He was adept at identifying himself, at least for the time being, with other people's ideas, which he found much more interesting to write about than his own. This is why so many articles in the *Dictionary* have philosophers of all periods as their subject. There was much that Bayle did not cover (we have noted that there is no article on Plato), but nothing that he deliberately excluded, as witness the article 'Gymnosophistes' which deals with the Hindu fakirs. As with heretics, Bayle makes every effort to do justice to the philosophers whose ideas he is summarising. Not having a personal axe to grind, he can afford to be objective. The extent of his documentation is astounding, and the only case in which he found sympathetic identification with a thinker's ideas impossible was that of the Jewish metaphysician Spinoza. Although original, even courageous, in his warm praise of the man, whom he upheld as the ideal type of virtuous atheist, he was guilty of a whole series of errors in the interpretation of his thought, through failing, in common with all his contemporaries, to come to terms with Spinoza's idiosyncratic vocabulary, in which traditional terms like 'substance' and 'attribute' are used in a very personal way. On the other hand, in the article 'Rorarius' in particular, he displayed a keen sense of the importance of his contemporary Leibniz (1646–1715), although Leibniz had only published a few articles and Bayle was incapable of understanding his mathematical writings. Finally, Bayle made connections between ancient and modern philosophers which are always stimulating even if sometimes specious. He realised in advance of his time that there is not an infinite number of metaphysical theses, and that there are 'family resemblances' between them which span the ages and cut across cultural boundaries.

Hand in hand with Bayle's devotion to the ideal of expounding other people's ideas as accurately as possible, and his pleasure in discussing their strengths and weaknesses, there went the belief that he lacked both the vocation and the ability to elaborate a doctrine of his own, or even to give wholehearted support to anyone else's (apart from Cartesianism in the broadest sense of the term, such as includes Malebranche). This meant that he had no need to engage in defensive arguments, and that, like a nomad, he could make critical raids on territories which others had cultivated and then slip quietly back to his desert. His profound and often subtle – but always courteous – criticisms of other men's metaphysical systems are made in the name of inner coherence, or common experience, rather than from any theoretical standpoint, apart from that furnished by a limited number of Cartesian basic principles. It is in this sense that Bayle is a sceptic and, by the same token, not so much a philosopher in the traditional acceptation of the term, as an expositor of philosophical ideas, and thus a 'philosophe' in the sense the word was to have in the eighteenth century.

5 What Bayle upheld

Royal absolutism and anticlericalism

In practical matters, Bayle never failed to make decisive choices, even if this involved him in considerable personal difficulties. In France, 'New Catholics' found themselves showered with financial benefits, and had Bayle continued to be a Catholic after his 1669 conversion, or had he returned to the fold later, as his Parisian correspondents kept urging him to do, he would have stood to gain considerably in material terms. Again, had he kept to matters of pure erudition and said nothing about his political views, he would never have come into conflict with Jurieu.

Had Bayle stayed in France, one might have wondered whether his championship of absolutism really represented his own sincere and considered views, since any other doctrine would have been suspect to the authorities. Absolutism, however, must have been very close to his heart for him to have espoused it so vigorously as a member of the Refuge, to which it was almost anathema. Bayle was not the only refugee to maintain the traditional Calvinist position, but most of the others prudently refrained from committing their views to paper, whereas Bayle put forward his with militant fervour and lack of caution. He is no less aware than any other Huguenot of the enormous drawbacks of an absolutist political regime. But, as often, it seems to him a matter of choosing the lesser of two evils: it is his belief that, in France at least, any other political system would have even more harmful consequences. The greatest benefits one looks to a political system to provide are order, security and civil peace. These are the necessary conditions for liberty, which is why Bayle does not begin by attaching primary importance to liberty itself, except in the matter of religion. It is pointless to think that one can increase one's liberty by weakening the authority of the central power: this will result either in the worst of all evils, civil war, or in the setting-up of petty local tyrannies which, in the end, because the governed are always literally under the eyes of the ruler, prove more arbitrary and more oppressive than an absolute monarchy. Bayle's attitude here should warn us against the anachronism of thinking that the new administrative order set up in the reign of Louis XIV was seen only as oppressive: on the contrary, to contemporary Frenchmen, especially in the distant provinces, it also spelled liberation from an inveterate state of chronic anarchy.

Following Hobbes (to whom the *Dictionary* devotes a substantial article), Bayle sees absolute monarchy as signifying the supremacy of the civil power and its independence from religious authorities, specifically the national clergy and the Vatican. Only an authoritarian, absolute monarch in France can be powerful enough to keep the tribe of ecclesiastics in their place. To this extent, of course, every Huguenot was bound to be anticlerical. If Bayle's anticlericalism made him seem more of an unbeliever in French eyes than did his 'paradoxes', it was because his French readers projected their own mentality on to what they read, to the point of forgetting that the author was not a Catholic, and inevitably found it impossible to conceive that such a frank and unremitting display of hostility and suspicion towards clerics could be compatible with belief. This was to overlook the fact that, while a Catholic happily submits to the tutelage of his priests, it is the Bible which is the oracle of the Huguenot, for whom the invisible Church, which is an object of faith, is quite distinct from the visible Churches, which (even if they are Reformed Churches) are fallible human institutions. Everything that Bayle experienced, first in France and then in Holland, encouraged him to draw a distinction between Christianity and the Churches that was unthinkable to a contemporary Catholic. Hence he can engage in swingeing criticism of theologians (including Protestant theologians whose own intolerance and fanaticism he never fails to point out) without calling the Gospel into question. Naturally, he does not deny that the clergy, of whatever confession, have their own legitimate sphere of action, which is to preach the Word of God and administer the sacraments. He also recognises that religious bodies have the right to exclude or excommunicate dissidents.

He hopes, without counting on it, that ecclesiastics will come to act in a spirit of mutual tolerance or something approaching ecumenism, but what he categorically rejects is the validity of clerical authority in secular and political matters, for example in civil legislation. Although the idea of the separation of Church and State was inconceivable to Bayle's generation, he went as far as he could in insisting that the State must ensure that the Churches confine their activities to the spiritual domain, while at the same time taking care not to let the imprecations of ecclesiastics intrude upon its own conduct of civil affairs.

In Bayle's eyes, the majority of clerics are characterised not so much by venality as by the lust for power. They use their position to make the masses into a docile but at the same time formidable tool by encouraging their tendency to superstition and by inciting them to fanaticism. In an abominable betrayal of their trust, instead of serving God they make Him serve them, and instead of fostering love of one's neighbour in their charges, they incite them to violence and rebellion. In the Wars of Religion, memories of which still lingered on, Bayle finds numerous examples of clerics urging Frenchmen to kill one another. And while the Catholic clergy are his main target, he does not exclude Protestant clergymen from his almost unending list of the cruel and immoral acts inspired by fanaticism. As for the polemics, of Homeric dimensions, to which the notorious *rabies theologica* has given rise, once again the *Dictionary* cites many examples on the Protestant side (and incidentally provides Bayle with a ready pretext to strike a blow, directly or indirectly, at Jurieu).

The proper spheres of the temporal and the spiritual

We are now in a better position to understand the sense in which Bayle can be termed an absolutist. The rights he ascribes to the ruler may seem exorbitant in modern eyes, but in Bayle's view they are the only way to make the supremacy of the civil power secure against powerful clerical adversaries, whose attempts to usurp sovereignty can only be thwarted by concentrating it in a single person. It is also important not to forget that when Jurieu, in his *Pastoral Letters*, upheld the right of popular resistance to monarchs who became tyrants, what he was advocating was not a democracy but a theocracy — in Bayle's eyes the most dangerous of all regimes since it is the one which gives the most power to clerics. Nor is Bayle's praise of absolutism at odds with his championship of toleration. He interpreted the Revocation as an indication not so much that Louis XIV was exercising power despotically, as that he was failing to enforce his absolute authority: it was the action of a bigot under the thumb of his confessor, not that of a king making his own decisions. In any case, Bayle was only being realistic in refusing, in the light of history, to believe that religious pluralism was possible in France on any other terms than under the aegis of undivided royal authority.

Anticlericalism implies that there can be no State policy that is 'holy', no crusades — and, more precisely, that all Scripture has to say on this subject is contained in the distinction between the things that are God's and the things that are Caesar's, and in Paul's statement in Romans 13 formally enjoining men that it is their duty to submit to authorities. There is a radical breach between the religious domain, concerned with the supernatural destiny of the individual, and the political domain, confined to the things of this world and to matters of public conduct. The social ethic, unlike the Gospel ethic, does not proscribe avarice, envy or egoism, takes no heed of intentions and prohibits only those actions that are openly harmful to others. Only in the exceptional case of the ruler is there a link between the two ethics. The ruler may be exempt from having to render an account of his actions to anyone on earth, but he will be held responsible for them before the tribunal of a God who, by laying on him the duty of ensuring justice and peace in his domain and forbidding him to go back on his word, obliges him to respect the 'fundamental laws' of his kingdom, which he swears to uphold in his coronation oath. The Christian monarch, as envisaged by Divine Right absolutism, can therefore never be confused with an arbitrary and capricious despot.

A static philosophy of history

Like everyone else in his day, Bayle believed that there was such a thing as 'human nature', always and everywhere the same beneath the infinite variety of customs. Similarly, like many humanists of the previous century, he did not think of human history as progressing, but as subject to perpetual cycles of prosperity and regression which affected each region of the planet in turn. While he was more than happy to have been born in Europe at an epoch when literature and the arts were flourishing, he had no doubt that eventually this would be succeeded by another period of 'gothic' darkness and barbarism. (When Bayle sided with the Moderns in the notorious Battle of the Books, it was only the initial, aesthetic aspect of the dispute that he considered.) It is particularly difficult for us today to enter into the mentality of people like Bayle, to whom the ideas of evolution, progress or even the reality of change were so alien, and who were deeply convinced that there was nothing new under the sun. But we must make the effort, if we are to understand fully some of the root causes of Bayle's pessimism. The iniquities he sees everywhere, the wretched existence most men lead, the abominable crimes with which history is filled, are for him ineluctable facts of the human condition, which is permanently at the mercy of famine, pestilence and war. Man has been, and is, just as unhappy and as wicked as he always will be. The corollary of this vision of life is a social conservatism which is aggravated by the conviction that any change is much more likely to be for the worse than the better. The established order is seen as a good, out of horror at the thought of the even worse state that might replace it. Moreover, the only alternative to holding that, on a global scale, the condition of humanity does not change, would be to maintain that it has been in steady decline since some far-off Golden Age. If men did change, it could only be for the worse.

Bayle's pessimism is all of a piece with his moral earnestness, and is the consequence of the disparity he perceives between what should be and what is. To take just one example, whereas men should live together in peace, what actually happens is that pride, greed ambition and the insane desire for 'glory' on the part of the rulers make the scourge of war endemic. Bayle describes

> the joy which whole nations feel when they learn that their soldiers have killed 200,000 men and laid waste ten provinces by fire and the sword, sparing no one regardless of sex, age or condition, and leaving to die of hunger in the woods and the caves anyone who has escaped their barbarity. When this news comes through, a whole population rejoices: everywhere there are festivities, bonfires, church bells ringing, artillery salutes, illuminations, songs, dances and fervent prayers that such exploits will be repeated. (*RQP* ii lxxii)

The relationships between European States are based entirely on force, being directed by a combination of violence and dissimulation, which to anyone who is the least bit perspicacious is clearly visible beneath the pompous rhetoric in which they clothe their official justifications for entering into conflict with one another. Bayle's own lucidity is partly the result of the long spells he spent outside his native land, whose political cynicism he clearly perceived, but to which he remained emotionally attached and so immunised against the slogans of hostile propagandists. As a result, he was never duped, as Jurieu was, into thinking of the policies of William of Orange as more idealistically motivated than those of Louis XIV.

Civil toleration and freedom of conscience

Along with a determination to avoid confusing the proper spheres of temporal and spiritual authority must go the acknowledgement that the political authorities have no need, and for that matter no right, to assume the direction of a nation's religious convictions. Bayle, it is worth recalling, holds that an individual's opinions have no influence on his conduct, and that the received notion that atheism is the source of all vices is disproved by experience: 'speculative' atheists like Spinoza are contemplatives, and the most peaceable of men, while practical atheists are shallow and boastful, atheists only because they are depraved, not depraved because they are atheists. If the civil power, whose task it is to maintain peace and order, has nothing to fear from atheists, then it has still less to fear from heretics. This is the real point of Bayle's argument, which he has prudently, and cleverly, presented in its most general form.

Bayle wanted the civil power to leave atheists in peace, and at the most only to forbid them from actively propagating their ideas. For heretics, however, he asked for at least the measure of freedom of worship and expression the Huguenots had enjoyed under Mazarin (1642–61) and the Roman Catholics now enjoyed in the United Provinces. How does he justify this distinction between atheists and heretics? The answer can be found by considering the metaphysical and religious context in which he developed his theory of freedom of conscience.

Bayle begins by posing the problem in its most general terms. He considers the case of someone with an 'erring conscience', without specifying the particular speculative errors that may be involved. In the seventeenth century there were three kinds of widely received argument which were used to justify the need for force in order to part such a man from his mistakes. The dissident was said to be a danger to the community whose members he might contaminate, hence he should be treated like someone who had the plague. He was said to be causing harm to himself, so that it was a matter of charity to save him, by constraint if need be, in the same way one prevents children from hurting themselves. Finally, heresy is an offence against God, and concern for God's reputation, which should always be active in a good Christian, requires the latter to chastise the blasphemer. The heretic was compared to an arsonist, a poisoner of wells, and a counterfeiter. Accused of divine *lèse-majesté*, he laid himself open to the harshest penalties promulgated by Mosaic law and by the legal system of the Late Empire. This accounts for the fact that so many contemporaries actually applauded Louis XIV for his 'clemency' towards the Protestants, who were, it is true, rarely put to death, being much more frequently sent to the galleys, deported or imprisoned for life, losing their worldly goods in any of these eventualities. Finally, to the list of arguments in favour of persecution there must be added St Augustine's interpretation, which had become traditional, of the words 'Compel them to come in' from the parable of the marriage feast in Luke 14:23. It was thus quite obvious to public opinion – it was, indeed, a commonplace of European thinking – that one of the essential duties of the secular arm was to extirpate heresy, or nonconformity, and to do so by force if need be.

Nowadays only two of the series of reasons by which our ancestors justified persecution still seem intelligible to us. One is the utility a community is supposed to derive from expelling its deviant members. The other is the duty of obedience to a god (nowadays represented by race, nation, 'Western civilisation' or 'the party line'). What we have particularly to understand is that men of the seventeenth century were deeply imbued with an altruistic concern for the eternal salvation of anyone who strayed from the fold. In combating the idea of intolerance, Bayle was involved in a much more complex task than if he had been simply laying down moral truths for the benefit of an opponent who was not worth arguing with. Instead he is often taking on St Augustine, whose approval of the use of force against the heretical Donatists had given Christians their excuse to indulge in persecution. The high level of the discussion in the *Philosophical Commentary* bears witness to this.

The first point Bayle contests is that religious uniformity is essential to a State. This he attacks as a circular argument. If intolerance is taken for granted, then clearly the civic loyalty of dissidents is undermined and they do constitute a potential danger to the country, since naturally they look for support to their co-religionists in foreign countries (as the Huguenots did to Elizabeth of England in the sixteenth century). However, as the example of the United Provinces shows, once the State no longer upholds intolerance, religious pluralism is possible without any harm resulting: Dutch Catholics for example, did not betray their country when the French invaded it in 1672. What is more, where there is religious pluralism, the various groups vie with one another to show that they are the better citizens, and the king is in a strong position as the arbiter between them. Since religious persecution is manifestly neither the only, nor indeed the best or even the cheapest, way of securing the loyalty of a people, it is more expedient to employ civil toleration to achieve this.

Bayle emphatically refutes the argument that to remove a heretic from the way of eternal damnation by offers of rewards or threats of punishment is an act of Christian charity. Adherence to a religion implies inner conviction, and inner conviction cannot be acquired under constraint. To offer rewards to anyone who will make a profession of orthodoxy is to encourage hypocrisy and self-interest, while the threat of punishment is not likely to make a heretic any more convinced of the truth of the religion which employs it. It is incongruous to try to enforce the religion of justice and charity through threats and bribes. The maxim 'Compel them to come in' has nothing to do with the use of force; it only urges us to invite others, lovingly, to seek the light. To the argument that it is obligatory, and indeed legitimate, for any orthodox believer to try to compel a heretic to adopt his creed, Bayle replies that, since every Church believes in its own orthodoxy, it would therefore follow that violence is legitimate whenever two different versions of Christianity clash, and indeed when used against Christians by infidels or, retrospectively, by the Roman Emperors.

The 'hard' champions of intolerance had one more argument left. Dissidents are blasphemers, and their punishment is called for by divine law. Bayle inverts the argument. Blasphemy does not lie in what is said, but in the intention behind it. Since the dissenter firmly believes that his 'errors' are true, his persistence in them is a tribute rather than an offence to the Divinity. 'The law that forbids a man to blind himself to the light of his conscience is one from which God can never dispense us since, if He were to do so, He would be permitting us to scorn or to hate him' (*Phil. Comm.* II viii). Persecution is crime because it goes against a supreme virtue, that of obeying God rather than man, and putting the dictates of conscience above worldly self-interest.

Thanks to his unusual approach, Bayle's solution to the problem of toleration is the opposite of the one usually found. He does not try to deny that heretics are in error so far as doctrine is concerned, but he argues that their error may be invincible, and hence innocent, in which case God is only concerned with the extent to which each individual has been true to the dictates of his conscience.

A keen collector of old medals may believe that he has a fine collection when most of them are forgeries, but no one would ever doubt that his devotion to his hobby is just as great as that of someone else who is equally keen but has been clever enough to purchase only authentic specimens. The two may differ greatly in intellect and acumen, but not in their passion for old medals. (*Phil. Comm.* Supplement, xviii)

Bayle, it should be recognised, is not an indifferentist. Not all errors can be thought of as innocent: they must be free of sloth and malice. Even so, only He who searches the loins and the hearts of men can tell infallibly if an error is innocent or not. Conscience, being the voice of God within each of us, is sacred, and the real offence against the Divinity is to persuade a man to forsake what his conscience tells him is true – and therefore, for him, *is* true. This Bayle regards as so important a point that he would rather see a heretic put to death than forced to abjure by threats of punishment or offers of rewards. At first sight, this may seem strange. But from Bayle's point of view, the man who denies his inner convictions out of fear or greed is putting his immortal soul in danger. Underlying Bayle's attitude there is too his personal revulsion for the deliberate infliction of physical or mental torture on another human being, such as his brother Jacob had suffered daily throughout five long months.

What Bayle upholds, then, is not the toleration of a particular idea, but respect for the human individual and the principle of freedom of conscience, of which civil toleration is the necessary condition. That his is an essentially religious attitude can be gauged from the fact that what makes conscience sacrosanct is the individual's apprehension of the rights of God over His creatures. Although atheists should, in his view, enjoy complete freedom in other respects, the fact that their attempts to make converts are not motivated by a divine command makes it legitimate for the civil power to prevent them from doing so. To put matters in another way, Bayle sees rights as something which the individual has only indirectly; what he has directly are duties, the most important of which is obedience to his conscience. Although written before the *Philosophical Commentary*, Locke's *Letter on Toleration* was printed after Bayle's work, anonymously and in Latin. The two great theorists of civil toleration, who were to exert so great an influence in the eighteenth century, conceived their ideas independently of one another. So far as practice is concerned, their views are very similar. The civil power has the right to regulate the external behaviour of the citizen, but not to attempt to control his inner convictions. Both further agreed in urging the Protestant rulers of Europe to be wary of Roman Catholics, while allowing them freedom of worship, on the grounds of their allegiance to a foreign ruler, the Pope. Their reasons, however, were appreciably different, Locke's being based on the rights of the individual and Bayle's on the rights of God. The religious tonality of Bayle's arguments is much stronger than in Locke. Again, as we have seen, it is not freedom itself that is the supreme good in Bayle's eyes, but order and civic harmony, which are the necessary antecedent conditions of freedom. Haunted by his knowledge of the Wars of Religion, Bayle was hostile to the idea of a social contract and the theories of the monarchomachists. He was, however, influenced by Hobbes, whose concept of the state of nature was in accordance with his own pessimism about man. While Locke looks to the future and is the theorist of a victorious revolution, Bayle's eyes are turned to the past; what he is seeking is a theoretical basis for the religious pluralism which the Edict of Nantes, no longer operative, had for a time made possible in France.

Bayle resembles the Spiritualist 'left wing' of the Reformation in displaying a moral rigorism which in his case is based simultaneously on the imperatives of a rationalistic ethics (Natural Law) and on the altruism of the Gospel (which he found clearly expressed, in contrast to the uncertainty of its dogmas). In this way, he avoids the trap of relativism. The sacrosanctity of conscience may make the ideal of unanimous agreement on religious doctrine unattainable, but it presumes such agreement where ethics is concerned: it founds an 'orthopraxis' rather than an orthodoxy. Bayle here refutes an objection he had anticipated: why should the persecutor be condemned, since he too is only following the dictates of his conscience? Bayle's reply is twofold. In the first place, justice and charity are self-evident rules of morality, as well as clear Gospel commandments, so that it is legitimate to doubt whether anyone who disobeys them can be said to have erred 'innocently'. In the second place, when they carry their intolerant beliefs into practice, the persecutors come under the authority of the civil laws, which exist to guarantee personal safety and public order, and they therefore invite punishment, not because of their inner convictions, but because they are troublemakers. The same thing had, of course, been said when English Catholics were harassed and when the Huguenots were punished for holding clandestine assemblies. Bayle, however, does not accept that the civil power has authority over peaceable assembly for religious purposes, whether it be to hear Mass, to sing Psalms, or to comment on the Koran (not that this was likely to be an issue at the time!). If Europeans claim the right to try to Christianise the whole planet, they must allow others an equal right to send their missionaries to Europe. The only occasion on which it is legitimate for the civil power to intervene in religious matters is when violence results, in which case the aggressor must be punished regardless of what his motives may have been: 'in deciding which opinions the State should tolerate, the criterion should not be whether they are true or false, but whether they endanger public peace and security' (*Phil. Comm.* II v).

6 Conclusion

It is not easy to formulate any kind of conclusion about someone who so delighted in leaving questions open, adopted so deliberately flippant a tone, displayed his pessimism so cheerfully (life being much too tragic to be taken seriously) and wore his massive erudition as lightly as Bayle did. The basis of Bayle's thought is a strictly logical development of Descartes's rejection of traditional authority. By extending this principle to spheres from which Descartes himself had explicitly, and prudently, excluded it, Bayle gave it a subversive bearing. Truth, he held, is not a body of knowledge that can simply be handed down, by ancestors, priests or rulers. It is something one has to discover for oneself and make one's own, and this necessarily makes it subjective, finite and liable to the influence of ignorance and error. It has to be thought of as the object of a permanent quest, a goal that no human being can ever actually reach.

A moral rigorist, Bayle associated error with sin, as much as sin with error. The person who never throws off his childhood prejudices is guilty of sloth and malice: not to call in question the things we have been brought up to believe is, literally, a sin. At the same time, heretics are not necessarily sinners (though everyone in Bayle's day believed they were). They may be the innocent victims of error. Moreover, only God can tell what is an innocent error and what is a culpable one, and this deprives mere human beings of the right to act against the latter, while God, being merciful, can be relied upon to forgive the former.

Bayle's *Dictionary* is a graveyard of ideological systems, in which the author sometimes plays the part of devil's advocate and sometimes of jeering vandal. He dismantles totems, treats heterodox notions with impartiality, ridicules theologians and their anathemas, reveals the bankruptcy of received ideas, and yet leaves the foundations of morality intact. The Ten Commandments are rational precepts whether men believe that a divinity promulgated and enforces them or not. Similarly, the golden rule of reciprocity ('Do unto others . . .') means respect for your neighbour's conscience and shows up religious persecution as a monstrous aberration.

It is not only through his scepticism but also through his trenchantly expressed affirmations that Bayle destroys the ideological presuppositions and the social practice of the French classical age. Great writers often owe their achievement to a happy conjunction of influences, and Bayle is no exception. His Protestant upbringing made him much more predisposed towards individualism and towards a critical approach to intellectual problems than if he had been a Catholic. French Protestants were much less liable to blind respect for established order than their Catholic counterparts, having been brought up to believe in the spirit of free enquiry and in the priesthood of all believers, as well as having been constantly involved in violent, often satirical, encounters with Catholics. At the same time, Bayle was always something of a marginal figure in Protestant circles. He guarded his independence jealously and used it to analyse ideas and events from the standpoint of a detached and lucid enquirer. This 'nobody', low-born, poor and exiled as he was, gave French Protestantism (which Louis XIV imagined he had wiped out) a voice and a message which were to be heard throughout Europe. Karl Marx saluted in Bayle the last of the seventeenth-century metaphysicians, and the first of the eighteenth-century *philosophes*.

Critics habitually tend to equate an author's ideas with the area of their greatest ostensible influence. Bayle provides us with a striking example of how great the gap between the two actually is. His thought was still predominantly theological in orientation, and yet it proved critically powerful enough to breach many old-established bastions. What he says about philosophy in general applies equally well to his own: it is like 'those powders which are so corrosive that after consuming the festering part of a wound, they eat away the living flesh, bite into the bone and penetrate to the very marrow' (*Dict.* Acosta n. G). Criticism thus became, in the hands of the Philosopher of Rotterdam, an instrument so sharp that it destroyed the mental universe to which he himself still very much belonged.

Appendix: Bayle and English culture

Bayle could have read at first-hand only those English authors who wrote in Latin. Otherwise, his access to them was through French translations or, more usually, through the substantial reviews which appeared in refugee periodicals (both Henri Basnage de Beauval and Jean Le Clerc knew English). Despite this, one of the most novel aspects of the *Dictionary* was that it introduced so many references to Protestant and hence to Northern European authors, categories which the French in general and Moréri in particular habitually ignored. The articles on Hobbes and Milton are especially noteworthy, that on Milton, in accordance with the contemporary view of the author, being almost wholly concerned with his political writings and only referring in passing to his activity as a poet. When in the course of his polemics with Jean Le Clerc Bayle also discussed the ideas of the Cambridge Platonist Ralph Cudworth (1617–88) and the theodicy of William King, later Archbishop of Dublin (1656–1729), he could only do so on the basis of the quotations and summaries furnished by his adversary. Although he is one of the earliest French writers to mention Newton, he did so only fleetingly, relying on the testimony of the Genevan mathematician and astronomer Fatio de Dhuillier, who was an enthusiastic admirer of the English scientist. The *Principia* was bound to be a closed book to Bayle, and all he does is to register his astonishment that Newton accepts the idea of a vacuum which Descartes had declared to be impossible a priori. Contradictions of this kind between physicists whose eminence could not be doubted were of course meat and drink to a sceptic like Bayle.

Bayle does not seem to have taken the trouble to read Coste's translation of Locke's *Essay on Human Understanding*, which appeared in 1700. The unregenerate Cartesian in Bayle no doubt jibbed at the empiricism he knew he would find in Locke's work, and in any case it was theology rather than philosophy which interested him during his latter years.

One of the reasons why Bayle exercised such a strong influence on the early stages of the Enlightenment is that, thanks to Des Maizeaux, his works were more widely available in English than in any other language soon after their publication. There are echoes of Bayle in Swift, Mandeville, Berkeley, Hume, Sterne, Gibbon and doubtless many others. Later, Bayle's ideas influenced Emerson and Melville. There are monographs on all these points, but there has been no synthetic study of Bayle's impact on English-speaking authors, whereas excellent ones exist for France, Germany and Italy.

At its most general, the enormous influence of Bayle's writings on the European eighteenth century is partly due to creative misunderstanding on the part of readers who were imbued with deism, optimism (notably, the idea of progress) and utilitarianism. As a result, Bayle's ideas very often acquired a significance totally at variance with their original meaning. In France, for example, what was originally a dispute with Catholics came to be interpreted as an anti-Christian polemic, and the accusations of impiety and atheism which Bayle's own theological adversaries levelled at him were taken at their face value.

The history of ideas shows that, once removed from its original socio-historical context, and read as the vehicle of a universal message, a work exerts its greatest influence not through the mechanical repetition or the exact reflection of its ideas, but through the ambiguities, misconceptions and anachronisms which find their way into its interpretation. The posthumous influence of Bayle's ideas provides a particularly striking example of the workings of this law.

Further reading

1. Bayle's works

The following list of publications mentioned in the text is arranged chronologically.

1682 *Lettre sur la Comète (Letter on the Comet)*

1682 *Critique générale de l'histoire du calvinisme de M. Maimbourg (General Criticism of Monsieur Maimbourg's History of Calvinism)*

1683 *Pensées diverses sur la Comète (Miscellaneous Reflections on the Comet)*

1684 *Nouvelles de la République des Lettres (News of the Republic of Letters)*

1685 *Nouvelles Lettres de l'auteur de la critique générale (New Letters by the Author of the General Criticism)*

1686 *Ce que c'est que la France toute catholique sous le règne de Louis Le Grand (The True State of Wholly Catholic France in the Reign of Louis XIV)*

1686 *Commentaire philosophique sur ces paroles de Jésus-Christ 'Contrain-les d'entrer'; Où l'on prouve par plusieurs raisons démonstratives qu'il n'y a rien de plus abominable que de faire des conversions par la contrainte, et l'on refute tous les Sophismes des Convertisseurs contrainte, et l'Apologie que S. Augustin a faite des persécutions. (Philosophical Commentary on the words of Our Lord 'Compel them to come in', in which it is proved by demonstrative reasoning that nothing is more abominable than to make conversions by force, and in which all the sophistry of those who would do so is refuted, likewise the apologia made by St Augustine for persecution.)*

1689 *Réponse d'un nouveau converti aux lettres d'un refugié (Reply of a New Convert to the letters of a Refugee)*

1690   *Avis important aux refugiez sur leur prochain retour en France* (*Important Warning to the Refugees concerning their Impending Return to France*)

1692   *Projet . . . d'un dictionnaire critique* (*Project . . . of a Critical Dictionary*)

1696   *Dictionnaire historique et critique* (*Historical and Critical Dictionary*)

1701   *Éclaircissements sur certaines choses répandues dans ce Dictionnaire* (*Clarifications* to the second edition of the Dictionary)

1703   *Réponse aux questions d'un provincial* (*Reply to the Questions of a Provincial*)

1704   *Continuation des pensées diverses* (*Continuation of the Miscellaneous Reflections*)

1707   *Entretiens de Maxime et de Thémiste* (*Conversations of Maxime and Thémiste*)

There have been many French editions of Bayle's *Dictionary*, and several translations. For those in English, see below.

The rest of Bayle's writings were collected under the title *Oeuvres diverses* in four folio volumes. There were two editions, in 1727 and 1737. A photographic reproduction of the 1727 edition was published by Olms at Hildesheim in 1964–8, and is supplemented by a fifth volume in two parts (1982) containing a French version of some of Bayle's Latin works, together with pamphlets by his friends and enemies relating to the polemics in which he was involved.

There is a modern critical edition of the *Pensées diverses sur la Comète* edited by A. Prat (1910). A corrected version of this edition with updated critical annotation by P. Rétat was due to be published by Nizet in 1982. *Ce que c'est que la France toute catholique* has been edited with an introduction and copious notes by E. Labrousse (Paris, Vrîn, 1973).

Most of Bayle's letters were printed in Volume IV of the first edition of his *Oeuvres diverses* (1727). His letters to his family, very poorly edited, were included in the second part of Volume I of the second (1737) edition. References are in the form OD^2 I B, followed by the page and column reference. A number of letters have been published subsequently, often in learned journals.

2. *English translations*

There have been two English translations of Bayle's *Diction-naire historique et critique*. The first was the work of various Huguenot refugees who were not native speakers, and appeared in 1710 as *A Historical and Critical Dictionary*. This was reprinted in 1734, doubtless to compete with the *General Dictionary Historical and Critical*, which was the second translation; its first volume had been published in 1734 also. It contained Bayle's text 'interspersed with several thousand lives never before published ...', mainly lives of Englishmen. This enterprise, in its concern to keep Bayle up to date, can be considered a distant ancestor of the *Dictionary of National Biography*. This new material was translated into French by Chaufepié and published in this form at The Hague in 1750–6, with a number of new articles.

The *Pensées diverses*, under the title *Miscellaneous Reflec-tions, occasion'd by the Comet* ..., and the *Commentaire philosophique*, under the title of *A Philosophical Commentary on ... Luke XIV, 23* ..., had already been published at London in 1708.

Selections from Bayle's *Dictionary*, by E. A. Beller and M. du P. Lee Jr., were published by the Princeton University Press in 1952. This was followed by another anthology, *Historical and Critical Dictionary – Selections*, edited by R. Popkin and C. Brush, New York, Bobbs-Merrill, 1965. K. E. Sandberg, *The Great Contest of Faith and Reason*, New York, Ungar, 1963, is a brief anthology which is particularly valuable for the inclusion of material from other works than the *Dictionary*.

3. *Selected studies on Bayle in English*

Howard Robinson, *Bayle the Skeptic*, New York, Columbia University Press, 1931 (interprets Bayle in the sense indicated by the title).

L. P. Courtines, *Bayle's Relations with England and the English*, New York, Columbia University Press, 1938.

W. H. Barber, 'Pierre Bayle: Faith and Reason', in *The French Mind, Studies in Honour of Gustave Rudler*, ed. W. G. Moore and others, Oxford University Press, 1952. This pioneering article marked a turning-point in the interpretation of Bayle's thought.

The following studies form a group:

E. D. James, 'Scepticism and fideism in Bayle's *Dictionnaire*', French Studies, XVI (1962), 307–24.

H. M. Bracken, 'Bayle not a skeptic', *Journal of the History of Ideas*, XXV (1964), 169–80 (reply to James's article).

W. E. Rex, *Essays on Pierre Bayle and Religious Controversy*, The Hague, Nijhoff, 1965.

K. C. Sandberg, *At the Crossroads of Faith and Reason, An Essay on Pierre Bayle*, Tucson, University of Arizona Press, 1966.

C. B. Brush, *Montaigne and Bayle*, The Hague, Nijhoff, 1966.

M. Heyd, 'A disguised atheist or a sincere Christian? The enigma of Pierre Bayle', *Bibliothèque d'Humanisme et Renaissance*, XXXIX (1977), 157–65.

There are numerous references to Bayle in the work of Richard Popkin: (a) in his *History of Scepticism from Erasmus to Spinoza*, Berkeley, University of California Press, 1979, an enlarged version of a book first published in 1960;

(b) in various articles, some of which have recently been collected in the volume *The High Road to Pyrrhonism*, San Diego, Austin Hill Press, 1980.

Index